W.WEDGWOO

ROBIN H

A Life on the Humber

A Life on the Humber

Keeling to Shipbuilding

HARRY FLETCHER

With an Introduction by
L. T. C. Rolt

FABER AND FABER LIMITED

3 Queen Square, London

First published in 1975
by Faber and Faber Limited
3 Queen Square, London WC1
Printed in Great Britain by
Butler & Tanner Ltd, Frome and London

ISBN 0 571 10723 0

For Liz

Acknowledgements

This book would never have been written but for my daughter Audrey. It was her idea in the first place and it was she who assembled and arranged the material, found the photographs, coaxed, persuaded and even bullied information out of me and dealt with such troublesome matters as full stops, commas and spellings.

I must thank, too, her husband Colin who has patiently read the typescript so many times, listened to all our disputes and together with Marjorie Wilkinson typed the first draft and its many amendments. I am grateful to all three for undertaking the tedious task of proof-reading, and to Marjorie in particular for her constant encouragement and enthusiasm without which we should never have had the courage to go on.

I owe a very special debt of gratitude to the late L. T. C. Rolt who, in spite of failing health, insisted upon writing the Introduction and compiling Appendix I. This was the last piece of work he undertook and it is a cause of real sadness to me that he did not live to see the publication of the book. I count it a great honour to have his name associated with it.

Then I should like to express my appreciation to the many friends and acquaintances who have helped in the preparation of the manuscript. First I have to thank Mr Henry Williamson, manager of Richard Dunston's shipyard of Thorne, who has brought me up to date with recent developments there and Mr I. M. Walker, Area Engineer, British Waterways Board, Castleford who has been most helpful in the preparation of a map of the South Yorkshire canals.

Acknowledgements

Members of keel families in Stainforth and Thorne have been kind enough to lend me the photographs which add greatly to the interest of the text, and Mr Eian Massey has spent many hours and much care in bringing them up to the standard required for publication. I am also indebted to the Humber Keel and Sloop Preservation Society which has assisted me in obtaining three of the photographs. Wherever possible, I have listed acknowledgements for individual plates in Notes on the Plates at the end of the book. I apologize for omitting acknowledgements to photographs of which the sources are unknown.

I should like to acknowledge, too, Mr Maurice Colbeck, editor of *Yorkshire Life*; Mr Winston Halstead, editor of *Yorkshire Ridings*; and Mr Trevor Hill, editor of the BBC's former programme 'Home This Afternoon', for permission to reprint material already published. I am also indebted to Mr Geoffrey Winter, chief features writer of the *Yorkshire Post*, and Mr R. G. Roberts, director of Leisure Services, Humberside, for their assistance in finding photographs of the period.

I should also like to thank Mrs June Hall of Faber and Faber for making the business of publishing such a pleasure.

Finally I must not forget all the old Thorne keelmen and their wives of the Darby and Joan and Old Age Pensioners' clubs with whom I have spent so many happy hours sailing and re-sailing every inch of the rivers and canals in our part of Yorkshire: Nellie Parish and J. A. Himsworth of Stainforth, Catherine Ackroyd (*Lily* and *Crane*), Fred Bisby (*Golden Cross*), George Foster (*Day Star*), George Hinchcliffe (*Unique*), Jim and Mizpah Holt (*Drucilla* and *Hanley's Pride*), Gwendoline Pickersgill (Walker) (*Snipe 2*), Herbert and Luther Rhodes (*Unity*), Lily Taylor (*Iona*) and Eric Lister, lock-keeper at Thorne.

8

Contents

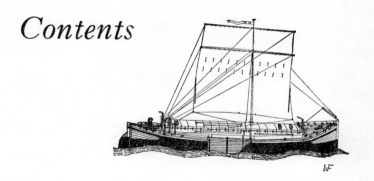

Acknowledgements   *page* 7
List of Illustrations   11
Map of the Area Showing the Author's Main Routes   13–14
Introduction by L. T. C. Rolt   15

1. *Keelboy*   19
2. *Waterway hazards*   39
3. *Keelmen and their families*   55
4. *Ashore*   67
5. *Plater's apprentice*   86
6. *The Depression*   112
7. *Shipbuilding again*   124

Appendix One by L. T. C. Rolt: Yorkshire Keel Canals
  and River Navigations   135
Appendix Two: Maps showing the Yorkshire Keel Canals
  and River Navigations   137
Notes on the Plates   141

Illustrations

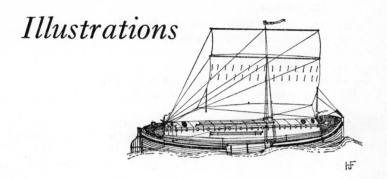

Notes on the Plates appear at the end of the book

1.	Keel *Sunbeam* on the Trent	*facing page* 16
2.	Keel *Attercliffe* at Keadby	17
3.	Keadby lock	17
4a.	The fore end of a wooden keel	32
4b.	Detail of the centrepiece decorated with gold leaf	32
5.	The *Faith* moored in Thorne 'rack'	33
6.	The wooden swing bridge at Stainforth	33
7.	The double locks at Keadby	48
8.	The Aegir on the Trent	48
9.	The tugs *Welshman* and *Irishman*	49
10.	The bridgeman's lobby at Toll Bar Bridge, Thorne	49
11.	A keelman's wedding	64
12.	The *Day Star*	64
13.	A horse marine taking his horse to the stables	65
14.	The Old House lock, Tinsley	65
15.	Stainforth Aquatic Sports Committee	80
16.	Sculling race for keelmen's wives	80
17.	The greasy pole	81
18.	Keels moored at Stainforth during Fair Week	81
19.	Thorne Travis Charity School	96
20.	Albert Dock, Hull	96
21.	The 'old harbour', Hull	97
22.	Rank's flour mill near the entrance to Victoria Dock on the river Hull	97
23.	The author's father, 'Young Jim', with a friend	97
24.	The author aged 18	112

Illustrations

25. The author's future wife, Liz, aged 18   112
26. Unemployed in the Depression   112
27. The oil tanker barge, *Snipe*   *facing page*   113
28. The *Maureen Eva*   113
29. Tom Puddings on the canal at Stainforth   128
30. The sideways launching of a large Tom Pudding at Dunston's   128
31. Staniland's keelbuilding yard at Thorne   129
32. The author aged 65 at the Yorkshire Dry Dock Company Yard   129
33. The author aged 75 with Dunston's in the background   129

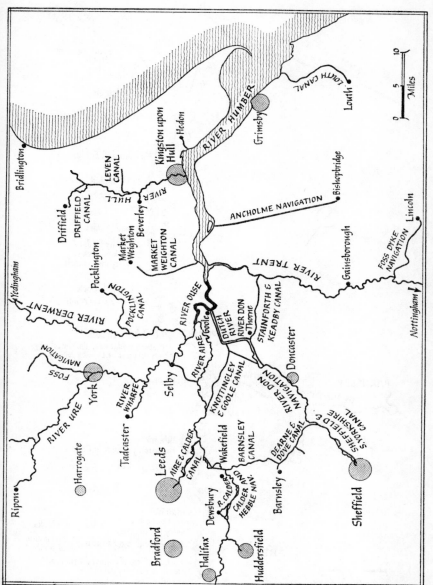

General Map of the Area

13

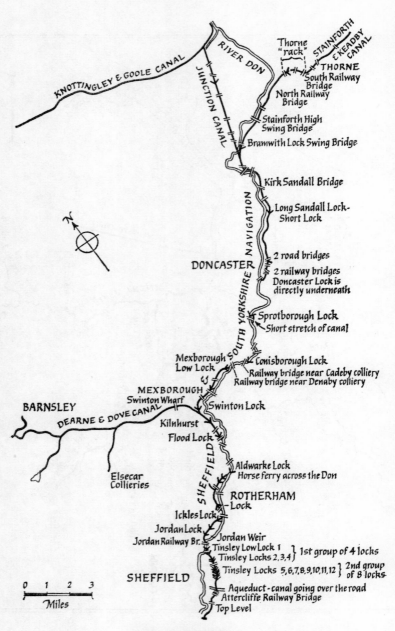

KNOTTINGLEY & GOOLE CANAL

RIVER DON

JUNCTION CANAL

Thorne "rack"

STAINFORTH & KEADBY CANAL

THORNE

South Railway Bridge

North Railway Bridge

Stainforth High Swing Bridge

Bramwith Lock Swing Bridge

Kirk Sandall Bridge

Long Sandall Lock-Short Lock

SOUTH YORKSHIRE NAVIGATION

DONCASTER

2 road bridges

2 railway bridges
Doncaster Lock is directly underneath

Sprotborough Lock

Short stretch of canal

Mexborough Low Lock

Conisborough Lock

Railway bridge near Cadeby colliery
Railway bridge near Denaby colliery

MEXBOROUGH

Swinton Wharf

BARNSLEY

DEARNE & DOVE CANAL

Swinton Lock

Kilnhurst

Flood Lock

Elsecar Collieries

Aldwarke Lock

Horse ferry across the Don

SHEFFIELD

ROTHERHAM
Lock

Ickles Lock

Jordan Lock

Jordan Railway Br.

Jordan Weir

Tinsley Low Lock 1
Tinsley Locks 2, 3, 4 } 1st group of 4 locks

Tinsley Locks 5, 6, 7, 8, 9, 10, 11, 12 } 2nd group of 8 locks

SHEFFIELD

Aqueduct - canal going over the road
Attercliffe Railway Bridge
Top Level

N

0 1 2 3
Miles

Harry Fletcher's Routes

Introduction
by L. T. C. Rolt

This is an autobiography of very unusual and many-sided interest. Mr Fletcher's working life may have been typical of many of those of his contemporaries on Humberside, but, so far as I am aware, not one of them has possessed the capacity to recall his life in such vivid and scrupulous detail.

His description of his childhood on board a Yorkshire keel is of the greatest value to anyone concerned with Britain's inland waterways. Thanks to the great revival of interest in these waterways, there have been many accounts of what life was like on the famous narrow boats of the Midland canal system, but of the Yorkshire keel and of those who worked them we have hitherto known virtually nothing. This despite the fact that, after the narrow boat, the keel was the second most numerous and wide-ranging class of inland waterway craft in use.

The canal age in England began in 1761 with the completion by James Brindley of the Duke of Bridgewater's Canal. But centuries before this date our English rivers had been used for the transport of goods. Navigation might be slow, difficult and subject to delays owing to flood or drought, but such hazards were tolerated in a country which was then almost devoid of metalled roads. A great variety of traditional types of sailing craft were used for this purpose and over the years these increased both in number and in range as river navigation was made easier or more extensive by the construction of locks and of many artificial cuts. Of all these regional types of river craft, the Yorkshire or Humber keel, operating on the network of Yorkshire rivers which empty into

the Humber, was almost certainly the most ancient. With its bluff
bows and square rig, the keel may well have been Norse in origin.
It certainly has the distinction of being the last craft in England
to carry a square rig, it being only thirty years since the last sailing
keel ceased to trade.

The improvement for navigation of the river Ouse to York was
authorized by Cromwell as early as 1657, while the rivers Aire and
Calder were made navigable to Leeds and Wakefield respectively
under an Act of 1699. From that date forward the Yorkshire river
navigations were gradually improved and extended. Yet, in every
case, from first to last, the size of the lock chambers on this
Yorkshire network of waterways was determined by the dimen-
sions of the keel, these being: length, 57–8 ft; beam, 14 ft 2 in–
14 ft 8 in; loading between 80 and 100 tons on the draft of 6 ft–
6 ft 9 in.

As the first appendix at the end of this book reveals, the extent
of these keel waterways ultimately totalled over 400 miles. It was
a system which undoubtedly played an enormous part in the
industrial development of the north-east, not only in the cloth
trade but in the coal and iron industries of south Yorkshire. It was
when it ceased to serve such a purely regional purpose but became
part of a national network, thanks to the efforts of James Brindley
and his successors, that it began to suffer from the lack of stan-
dardization, and this defect became a terrible handicap when canals
found themselves fighting against railway competition.

This fatal lack of uniformity was nowhere more apparent than
on the trans-Pennine routes. For the canals east of the Pennines
were all constructed to a gauge determined by Brindley with locks
to accommodate the famous narrow boat (70 ft long and 7 ft
beam) either singly or in pairs. Thus the Rochdale was a broad
canal which climbed over the Pennines from Manchester by great
flights of 70 ft × 14 ft 2 in locks until it made an end-on junction with the Calder and Hebble Navigation, with its short locks,
at Sowerby Bridge. An even worse example was the Huddersfield
Narrow Canal with its ladders of 70 ft × 7 ft locks leading to its
great summit tunnel at Standedge, the longest in Britain. For this
joined at Huddersfield with the Huddersfield Broad Canal which
was built to suit Yorkshire keels. The effect of this was that only
a shortened version of the narrow boat of 7 ft beam but only
58 ft long could use these canals as a through route. Such very

1. Keel *Sunbeam* on the Trent

2. Keel *Attercliffe* at Keadby

3. Keadby lock

small boats naturally had a very limited carrying capacity. In the face of such disastrous anomalies as this, the wonder is that the narrow boat and the Yorkshire keel should have survived in the face of railway competition on the trans-Pennine routes as long as they did.

Whereas the narrow boat survived into our own day and has been well recorded both in text and photograph, the earlier passing of the Yorkshire keel went virtually unrecorded and this is what makes Mr Fletcher's memories so valuable. For example, until I read his book I had assumed that, like other traditional types of river craft, the sailing keel was manned exclusively by men whose womenfolk lived 'on the bank'. I was therefore most interested to learn that, although the Fletcher family had a cottage at Thorne on the Stainforth and Keadby Canal, Mr Fletcher's mother usually accompanied his father on the keel. He gives us uniquely realistic and detailed accounts of what it was like to work and live on a sailing keel plying between the port of Hull and Sheffield in the years before the First World War; also, a minutely detailed description of the keel itself.

So hard was the life that young Fletcher understandably decided to give it up and got himself a job ashore as a plater in a Hull shipbuilding yard throughout the First World War. His account of this period, written 'from the shop floor', as it were, presents us with a very different though no less interesting slice of life.

I finished my engineering apprenticeship in the midst of the slump period between the wars, so I know just how difficult it was then for even a skilled man to obtain employment. But for those who did not have such first-hand experience, Mr Fletcher's account of these years make salutary reading. He tells us how his skilled employment in the shipyard soon came to an end in the dole queue and in a variety of unskilled and ill-paid jobs. This state of affairs continued until he finally found congenial skilled work in his old trade at a small shipyard on the banks of the Stainforth and Keadby Canal in his birthplace of Thorne. This was at the beginning of the Second World War and it was a sign of the times that this yard, which had once built wooden keels, should now be building steel barges and tugs. Such new steel craft traded over the same waterways that had once been built for keels but had since been greatly enlarged. At this period Mr Fletcher still saw passing the yard some of the old wooden keels, now no longer carrying their sails but fitted with diesel engines.

When I passed through the Calder and Hebble and the Aire and Calder Navigations in 1947 in the course of a voyage through the northern canals, I remember encountering quite a number of these old converted keels. But I was just too late to see one under sail. To see one of these ancient, traditional craft with its great square canvas set on its tall mast, sailing slowly and majestically along through the flat Yorkshire countryside must have been an unforgettable spectacle. Those of us who have been denied such a sight in reality will find Mr Fletcher's vivid memories the best substitute.

L. T. C. R.
March 1974

1 *Keelboy*

Most men looking back to their childhood remember a house and a garden. I remember boats and a river. I was born in July 1899, and by September of the same year was living aboard a keel in the middle of a canal. My father and both my grandfathers were keelmen, working boats on the Humber, the Trent, the Ouse and the canals of South Yorkshire.

Keels were sailing barges, supposed to be the direct descendants of Viking longships. When fully laden down to the decks they looked so heavy and cumbersome that the resemblance was hard to see, but when they were coming down the Humber with no cargo and in full sail there was no mistaking it.

The first keels were clinker built, with the lower edge of each plank overlapping the upper edge of the one below, like slates on a roof. In my father's time, however, they were all carvel built, smooth sided, their planks meeting, and on an oak keel. Their decks were of pine and their planks of larch. Their size depended on the locks and bridges on the different waters they had to use.

The majority of keels were painted blue or green, although some large firms had their own colours. One firm painted their keels red, and Furley's of Hull were always yellow.

The outsides of our keels were tarred or black varnished except for the top strake, the top planking round the keel, which was just scraped and varnished. The timberheads, the sheet heads and the hatch sides, called coamings, were painted a light blue until the keel was thirty years old, when the colour was changed to green. They were finished off with fancy work called stringing, a thin line border with a design in the corners, done in dark blue on blue keels and dark green on the green ones. It broke the monotony of plain painting, and looked most attractive when well done.

The pieces across the ends of the hatch, known as headledges, were grained like real wood, oak, pine, mahogany or teak. The feathering pieces on the bows were usually decorated with a spray of leaves done in gold-leaf on black. The name of the keel and that of the captain were painted in gold or white on the transom rail aft.

Keelmen were very proud of their painting. There were no set designs, no hearts or roses. Each man followed his fancy. I first helped Dad to paint when I was six or seven years old, and I remember Mother telling him he was gormless to let a lad of that age loose with a paint-brush as I used to get into such a mess. Still, I kept on, and by the time I was twelve I was quite skilful and helped my Grandad Fletcher as well as my Dad. They were both considered good hands at lettering, and said if I kept it up I should beat the lot of them, but all three of us had the same trouble—we could never get an S to look right, and to me even now, the S on professional signs often looks wrong.

I used to help to paint the boat while we were waiting for cargoes in the docks, and I liked to paint lifebuoys on the forecastle hatch with trawlers inside them. I had ships painted all over the forecastle, which I always said was mine.

My grandfather, nicknamed Lemon Bill, asked me to paint one on his hatch, and when I'd finished he said the trawler was going the wrong way. He always said whatever you do, always leave something for people to find fault with and they'll talk about it—otherwise you won't hear a word.

The trawler I chose was the North Sea trawler, the *Kestrel*, of the Pickering and Haldane Line. She was iron built, and in use in the early 1900s, so she was one of the earliest trawlers I remember. Her open deck was typical of trawlers of that period.

The paint we made ourselves by mixing coloured powder with boiled linseed oil and a very small amount of turpentine to help it to set. Keelmen always said that quick-drying paint would not stand the weather and the salt water of the Humber.

Gold-leaf came in thin sheets between tissue paper. First we gold-sized the parts to which it was to be applied, then laid or pressed the leaf on with a soft brush. It stayed on only where it was in contact with the gold-size, but if you coughed or sneezed it would blow away, as it was so very thin (and so very expensive), but once on, it would stand the weather and the water. On windy days this painting had to be done in the cabin, or the precious gold would all have been lost.

We had paint-brushes of every conceivable size. Some had long handles for those parts of the boat we could not easily reach, and we used a small camel-hair one for the stringing patterns and the lettering.

The big square mainsail was white, always white and edged with rope to strengthen it. I have seen one coloured brown in a book called *Sailing Ships and Sailing Craft*, by George Goldsmith Carter (Hamlyn, 1969), but I never saw any but white in all my life. Some keels had a rectangular topsail too, also white. We used to swing the whole rig round to lie lengthways along the boat when we were in narrow locks and canals, and in that way it cleared all obstructions. When not in use the sails were rolled up on the yard-arm and covered by a tarpaulin made especially for the job. Sloop sails were tanned brown or red to preserve them but they were never covered up, as ours were, when not in use.

At the top of the mast we flew a flag called a 'vane' because it acted as a weather vane to show us which way the wind was blowing. It was 4 in wide, on a narrow wire frame for about 18 in and the rest was 2 or 3 ft of bunting.

It was quite different from the 'burgee', which was the flag with the keel's name on it. The burgee was 14 ft long but was only flown at the launch or on special occasions, like the water sports or regattas. It was usually given to the keel's owner after the launch and kept in a locker—although there was one yard on the Humber which always charged for the burgee, a fact that we all remembered.

All keels had leeboards, pear-shaped pieces of wood about 10 ft × 6 ft, fixed to the side of the boat in line with the masts. They were lowered into the water to help sailing when we had to tack in a head wind.

We also had a little rowing boat called a coggy boat which we towed behind the keel in the Humber just in case the keel sank. Keels easily turned over if caught broadside on when fully loaded, and the coggy boat was so fastened that it could be released immediately in an emergency. There was so little of the keel above water when it had a good load that in a collision it could sink in a matter of minutes. Sometimes we had as little as 18 in at each end, and no freeboard at all amidships, which were often awash.

The coggy boats were built at the same time as the keels and were usually of larch or elm. They had a square stern and were sculled by a single oar. I have heard that the word 'kogge' is even older than the Vikings, and was given to a little boat in Frisland where there was a seafaring people as early as the first century A.D. Apparently the Vikings copied these cog boats before they perfected their longships round about A.D. 800.

We always carried two anchors and two anchor chains, about 30 fathoms of chain in each, for use in the Humber and the Trent. They were no use in the canals.

Keels like ours were made in boatyards all over South Yorkshire. Dunston's in Thorne have been making boats for over a hundred years, and they started with keels. Staniland's, another boatyard, made its last keel as recently as 1922.

A keel cost about £450 and many captains bought their own by paying a deposit and working off the balance from their earnings. It took them fifteen to twenty years to clear the debt, depending on how well they managed to get cargoes.

My father never owned his own keel. He worked for a carrying agent called Wilson who owned five or six keels, and he was a captain for them—a keelman in charge of a keel was always known as captain—before he was twenty. His first keel was the *Irene*, one of the first iron-built keels.

He left Wilson's to become the captain of the *Mary Ward*, a wooden keel 64 ft long and 16 ft 3 in broad with a stem of 7 ft. She was the boat I remember best. She belonged to a cripple who lived next door to us in Thorne, for although we lived aboard most of the time, we always had a house in Thorne as well. Mother always stayed at home to have her children and both I and my younger brother were born in Thorne. My father worked the keel for our neighbour because he had lost the use of both legs and was unable to work at all. That meant that this particular keel had to keep two families instead of one, and consequently we were always hard up.

It was the captain's job to find a cargo. First he went to the carrying agents on the dockyard in Hull to find general cargo, then to the coal agents for a commission to pick up a load at one of their particular collieries.

Occasionally the agents went looking for keels, but this only happened when a family owning several keels had too much cargo for their own fleet, and had to ask a captain who owned his own keel to help them out.

General cargo, consisting of peas, sugar, liquorice, tinned fruit, machinery and even clothes-pegs, was collected from the town docks and carried inland to Doncaster, Swinton or Mexborough. Our keel could carry 76, 90 or 110 tons, depending on the depth of canal we were using.

From the Victoria Docks in Hull we picked up timber to be used as pit props in the collieries, and which had been carried in the bottom of ships from Norway, Sweden and Russia to counteract the deck cargo. Iron ingots from Norway and Sweden, and white sand for glass- and steel-making we took to Sheffield and Tinsley. Wheat, maize and oats we loaded from the Alexandra Docks for transport to the flour mills in Doncaster, Sheffield and Mexborough.

The coal we collected from the colliery towns for our return journeys always went to St. Andrew's Dock, the fish dock, where we had to go into an extension known as Klondike and wait until a trawler on contract for coal to our particular agent arrived. Discharging coal into the trawler was done by hand, and Dad always had to help or pay a man to do it for him at a charge of 1½d a ton. The usual rate of discharge was 10 tons an hour, so that the filler could earn 15d, but it was hard work, especially when you first started and the coal was level with the hatch tops. You had to dig straight down until you reached the bottom of the hold, called the 'shuts', shovelling the coal as you went. This was called 'digging shuts' and I've done it many a time. After that the work was easier because you just had to dig along the hold to the aft end of the keel: 'filling out' we called that.

There were usually two men unloading, one on each side of the keel, shovelling the coal into baskets, eight to a ton. The baskets were heaved up on rollers by another two men, and a fifth tipped and stowed. The sea-going trawlers had to carry as much coal as possible for their long journeys to the White Sea, and they sometimes carried it even on their decks.

Occasionally we took a cargo of 'washed slack', coal soaked in water and weighing 21 cwt to the ton. We pumped out five or ten tons of water during the journey, and were only paid for carrying 20 cwt at the docks, but that was better than no cargo at all. The trawler owners preferred 'washed slack' to 'bright hards', which was hard steam coal. Soft house coal was no use in boilers and 'bright hards' burned too swiftly, and was uneconomical.

The only unusual cargo we ever carried was 110 tons of seed potatoes from a farm near Medgehall. They went on the Wilson Line ship *Marengo* for export to America.

Waiting for the next cargo was our biggest worry, and it was expensive too, as we were never paid for all the time we wasted either at the collieries or at the docks. Sometimes we waited for days, perhaps more than a week, for a load of coal, and then we had to wait again at the fish docks to discharge it into the trawlers. Then there would be yet another wait while Dad found a cargo for our return trip. If we could not get a cargo at either end, it meant we had to make the return journey empty, or 'light', and no cargo meant no money. Apart from the expense, waiting was boring, for we were sometimes moored up for three or four weeks.

As a boy I spent the time playing football if there were other boys around. Once we had a match on the ice at Roundwood. We put brushes up for goal posts, and I was goalkeeper at one end. It was a rough game and there was at least one broken leg at the end of the afternoon. Sometimes we had a go at boxing, or we just sat and watched the Norwegians unloading their herrings during the season.

I was watching when the trawlers that had been fired on by the Russian Navy came in from sea. These trawlers were 'boxmen', or 'fleeters', because they sailed in a fleet and packed their catch into boxes, transferring it at about four o'clock in the morning to a carrier ship which took it straight to London. They always fished at night by the light of acetylene lamps, and the Russians had seen the ships and the flashing lights and thought the Japanese fleet was attacking them. They opened fire and had killed two fishermen before they realized their mistake. In the Boulevard at Hull there is a monument to these two men, and to a third who died of shock later.

We spent a lot of our time catapulting at rats under the landing-stages. They were the biggest I have ever seen, as big as large cats, and at night when we were in bed we could hear them running about the decks. We had to take care they didn't get into the keel. Occasionally they did and we had to put down poison for them. I remember once seeing Mother going to the cupboard for a toy for my baby brother and putting her hand on a dead rat instead. She was up that ladder and out of the cabin hatch quicker than I could ever have been.

We liked to fish too. In the docks we were allowed to fish from the keel but not from the land. I caught codlings, whitings, flatties, eels and smelts, all good to eat, as they were salt-water fish.

In the evenings we read or listened to the phonograph, which played cylindrical records made of wax which broke immediately if we dropped them. They were played with a sapphire needle, and were chiefly music-hall songs like 'Won't You Come Home, Bill Bailey?' or 'My Girl is a Highborn Lady'.

But in spite of all these amusements, hanging about was boring, and I didn't like it. It seemed stupid to me to have nothing to do for weeks, and then to have to work really hard for sixteen or even eighteen hours a day.

When we did finally load up and set off on our journey, it was always up the Humber. Wherever we were going or whatever we were carrying, we had first to pass through the dock gates into the river. On this stage of the journey we were usually pulled by steam-tugs which had their propellers in a tunnel in the bottom of the ship so that if they touched the bed of the river the blades did not break.

These steam-tugs picked us up outside the lockpits of the docks and towed as many as six keels at a time. They towed in two lines of three steered in a V-formation, so that each boat avoided the backwash of the one in front. They took us up the Humber to the mouth of the Trent and up that river as far as Keadby. They charged 10s for 30 miles and it took us about three and a half hours, depending on the weather and the tide. If the tide was running at 10 knots, or if a gale blew up, it could take considerably longer. Humber gales could reach 60 miles an hour with waves 6 to 8 ft high. There were times when both Mother and I had to be lashed to the mast to stop us being swept overboard. The tiller, too, had to be lashed to keep the keel on course. Gales of this force could stop almost all river traffic, and it was dangerous to try getting ships into docks. They just had to drop anchor and wait for calmer weather.

The steam-tugs were rarely used on the Sheffield and South Yorkshire canals, and on the Aire and Calder only for Tom Puddings, square floating containers fastened together like huge snakes. When we reached Keadby, therefore, we had to use the sail, which we generally put up in the river while we were waiting for the locks into the canal to fill. There was a double lock at Keadby, with one set of lock gates for when the water in the canal was higher than the Trent, and another set for when the Trent was higher than the canal.

There were times when we could not afford the steam-tugs and had to use the sail in the Humber too. Then we got it all ready in the lockpits while we were waiting for the tide to come up and the lock gates to open.

The mast was heavy, varying from 40 to 45 ft in length, and weighing between 5 and 6 cwt. It fitted into a square wooden socket called a lutchet, which was attached to the main beam, the one going across the keel, at deck level, and to the centre keelson, the inner keel running the length of the ship, below deck, so it was firmly held both at the bottom of the boat and at deck level. Below decks this lutchet was solid and tapered down to the bottom of the boat, but above deck it formed an open socket for about three feet, with one of its four sides open so that the mast could be raised and lowered.

When not in use, the mast lay in a depression along the centre of the hatches at the aft end of the keel, with its base in the lutchet. It had to be hauled into position whenever we needed it, and this was done by turning the forerollers which pulled the ropes and wire attached to the mast and heaved it into an upright position. When it was up, we put a bolt across the open side of the lutchet, and so the mast was firmly held.

Next we had to put up the sail. Sailing was an art, and each captain had his own ideas about it. If the wind was light, we hoisted both the big square mainsail and the smaller topsail. If the wind was stronger we left off the topsail, and if it was very strong, we took in two reefs in the mainsail. Every mainsail had two rows of ropes, called reef points, sewn in one above the other, and we could fold the sail around the main yard-arm and tie the ropes— the top or bottom row according to the strength of the wind. We also had a truss, a rope fixed to the back of the sail, divided into two like an inverted letter Y. The stem of the Y led up through the mast at the back of the sail and along to the aft rollers. By pulling up the truss we could reduce the width of the sail and slow ourselves down. We used it mainly in the canal when approaching a bridge or a lock, and when passing other keels. If we wanted to reduce speed in the Humber, we took in a reef.

Different types of wind required different methods of handling sails. Fair winds, straight along the length of the keel, were very easy: the sail had simply to be across the keel. In a beam wind, blowing across the keel we had to have the sail almost fore and aft; while in a shy wind, almost but not quite against the way you wanted to go, the sail had to be just slightly fore and aft. This also applied when tacking in a head wind on the Humber. Then we had to lower the leeboards and zigzag backwards and forwards at an angle against the wind, turning the sail completely every time we turned the keel. It was a complicated business. While one man managed the sails, the other had to run from one side of the keel to the other with a ten-foot sounding rod, to test the depth of the water before the keel could be swung in any direction. This manœuvre was, of course, impossible in a narrow canal, and with head winds there we had to haul by horse or by hand.

Sometimes you could sail a good distance, then the canal would turn and sailing became impossible, either because you had lost the wind or because the change of direction had made it a head wind. 'Head wind racks' these stretches were called. Another turn in the canal might soon make it possible to sail again. Canals had one or two such turns, so the captains had to know each canal thoroughly to decide whether it was worth sailing or not. They also had to know how many head winds they were likely to encounter on any particular stretch of canal.

'Thorne rack' was a well-known stretch of canal between the two railway bridges. If you had a good wind going to Doncaster, you certainly hadn't one coming back. You would often see the keelman's wife and his children strung out in a line along the hauling bank, and the eldest child to the smallest toddler pulling the keel with the man-line while the keelman steered and pushed with a boat-hook. Of course, the smallest weren't doing much pulling, but they were there.

If the wind dropped while we were sailing in the Humber, we simply had to wait and use the big oar, which was 12 ft long and fixed at the fore end of the keel. It was there so that we could at least keep control of the keel in a fast tide. We sat on the deck to row. The Vikings used to steer their ships in this way, too—or so I'm told.

Keels going up river by sail could only go on a flood tide and if that tide was running at 5–6 knots and our own speed through the water was 3–4 knots, then overall our speed was as much as 9–10 knots.

Of course, we couldn't sail as fast on the canals, although the keels had such lofty masts especially so that we could catch every breath of wind in the flat countryside through which we travelled. In any case the Canal Company stipulated a maximum speed of 3 mph to protect the hauling banks, though I must admit that no one lucky enough to get a good wind ever took any notice of it.

We usually sailed along the canal to Crowle, Medgehall and Thorne, but when sailing was impossible we had a man and a horse to pull the keel from the hauling banks. We hired the horse marine, as we called him, from the canal towns by sending word with a passing keel. In Thorne we hired Martin Henry, who had only one horse, and led it himself. In Mexborough we hired from a family called Bisby, who owned fifteen or twenty horses, and charged roughly 1s a mile.

Sometimes the same horse marine would take us right through to Sheffield. When we reached Mexborough he would stable his horse at the lock-keeper's cottage and sleep himself on the lockers in our cabin. There were times when I had to sleep like that myself. We used to say that Dad could sleep on a clothes-line. He could have done too, and woken up at the right time, for he could wake at whatever time he wanted without an alarm clock. I never could!

Part of the horse marine's fee was his breakfast or dinner aboard the keel. Mother cooked when she was aboard, but if she was not, it was my job. These men had such huge appetites that Dad used to say that they only ate when they were hauling our keels.

When the horse marine was hauling he often walked backwards at the canal side of the horse, to keep an eye on the keel and to make sure that the line did not foul anything, for if it had done, the horse would have fallen into the canal. The horse wore a strong but simple harness. It had a collar with a side trace at each side. These reached a little behind the horse, and were

28

fastened to a piece of wood called a cobble-stick, and made especially for keel-hauling. In the middle was a hook which swivelled either way, and to which the horse line was fastened.

The rest of the harness consisted of a back band, which went from the collar along the back of the horse and ended with a loop for the horse's tail. Two other back bands led downwards from this one and supported the traces. The horse had a bridle with short reins, and a halter so that we could tie him up and prevent him from wandering off or falling into the canal whilst we were waiting our turn at the locks. We fastened the horse line, a short cotton line, to the mast or to a short pole called a neddy, which fitted into the lutchet if the mast had been taken down.

The horses knew exactly what to do with a loaded keel. They went slowly into the line until it was tight and then just lay against the line as if they were lying down.

It took a horse eight hours or more to pull a keel 10 miles, so there was no stopping to eat. It ate as it worked, out of a nose tin fastened by a rope which went over its head and which could be adjusted to any height. We put corn and chaff into the tin and damped it down so that the horse could not blow the chaff away. The feed was carried on the horse's own back, in a long, narrow corn bag made of sailcloth. Often, after the poor creature had hauled for ten or eleven miles, it had to walk back with the horse marine riding so as to be ready for the next day's work, which meant a day of more than twelve hours for both horse and man.

The only change or rest it got was when hauling banks changed sides. At Kilnhurst on the river Don we had to hang on to the hauling banks while the horse was ferried across, but usually there was a bridge.

The horses had a poor time of it, and had a shorter life than most, for keel-hauling was a killing job. They were worked until their strength failed, then were sold to horse-dealers and put down, to end up as dog-food, fats and bone meal. I never heard of any being put out to grass or given honourable retirement.

Looking back, there was only one horse I remember very well. His name was Galloway, but we always called him Noddy, because he was always nodding his head. Strangely enough I don't remember the horse that bit me—but then its teeth only went through my coat sleeve.

I sometimes had to lead the horse, and it was a responsible job

29

for a boy. A big brown mare once trod on my foot when I was leading. I gave a great yell, but had to limp on to the next bridge before I could get a rest. The average speed of that horse was $1\frac{1}{4}$ miles an hour, but it seemed like two hours before it lifted its foot. Two of my toes were black when I took my boot off, and I really thought they would fall off.

Another time the horse missed its footing and rolled down the bank into the water. I was much too weak to stop it, and the banks were so steep that we could not get it out again, so we tied it to the back of the keel and towed it along. The journey was not without incident, and Dad had to stand some racket when we passed other boats.

'Hey up, Young Jim!' shouted one captain (since my dad was always known in this way even when he was in his sixties). 'Doesn't tha know tha's got t'horse at wrong end?'

The horse enjoyed it. There he was, having a cool swim while Dad pushed the keel with a boat-hook, the horse marine pulled from the hauling banks and I steered. The accident happened near Sandall but we reached Doncaster, about three miles away, before we found a flat spot to haul the horse out, and even then it took six men to do the job.

If times were bad and we couldn't even afford a horse marine, or we were having to take an empty keel back to Hull, then we pulled the keel by hand, using a harness called a seal, made of a piece of sailcloth or leather about 3 in wide, with ropes attached to each end. These were tied to a thin cotton line called a man-line, which was much lighter than a horse line. We put the seal across our chests and round our shoulders and leaned forward, getting as much weight as we could into the seal, and unlike the horse marine, we faced the way we were going. Mother and I pulled when the keel was empty, and could move it at a walking pace.

Sometimes we even used a boat-hook to get us along. We put the end with the hook on anything handy—another keel, a wall, the bottom of the canal—and then we pushed. We had two or three boat-hooks of different lengths, with a hook and a prong at one end and a pummel at the other. The pummel was about 3 in in diameter, and we put it against our shoulders and pushed or pulled by gripping the boat-hook with both hands.

Our progress along the canals, whether by sail, horse or hand, was always slowed up by the locks. The keel was lifted up twenty-eight locks between Hull and Sheffield, and old keelmen used to say that by the time a keel reached Sheffield it was as high as Holy Trinity Church in Hull. Whether that was true or not, the locks were hard work and took up a lot of our time. We usually worked one side of the lock while the lock-keeper worked the other.

If we were going up to Sheffield, the lock would be full of water, so the lock-keeper would heave up the clough, or sluice valve, on the lock gates. This opened a hole below water-level and let the water out into our side of the canal. When the level in the lock had gone down to the level of our side of the canal, we pushed open the lock gates and pushed or pulled the keel into the lock, closed the gate behind us and lowered the cloughs. The lock-keeper then went to the other gates and opened the cloughs, so that water poured into the locks and raised the keel 4–6 ft to the level of the far side of the canal. Then we pushed open the gates and went on our way. We always threw a penny on to the lock side for the lock-keeper to pick up, although he was officially paid by the Canal Company.

At Tinsley, where the canal climbed a hill, came our worst hold-up. This was a group of four locks and another of eight, only two of which had lock-keepers. At the other ten the keelmen had to work the locks themselves. It was a slow process. At the top was a lovely three-mile stretch into Sheffield, which we called the top level. Every time a keel went through the top lock, a whole lockful of water was lost, so to keep the water up to a working level water was pumped up from the river Don.

Another hazard on the canals, and one which slowed us up considerably, was the bridges. Whether they were swing or fixed bridges, they were great time-wasters. The swing bridges were usually opened by the wives of men employed by the Canal Company to mend the banks, dredge the water and cut the weeds and reeds. Their cottages were near the bridges, and when they heard our signal from the foghorn they would come out and push the bridge open so that we did not have to stop. They all had a little bag on a stick which they held out as we passed through, and Dad would put a penny in it. If you didn't, you probably had a long wait the next time you passed that way. Their wages were very low, and these pennies were appreciated, though each family generally had a vegetable garden, a few hens, a pig or two and sometimes even a cow which grazed on the canal banks and helped them to live.

Fixed bridges were more difficult. If the keel was empty, we had to unship all the fixtures above hatch level, and if that did not leave us enough room, we had to open the sea-cocks and flood the bottom of the keel, which was called the dennings. We could carry 20 tons of water in this way without flooding the hold or the cabins. Ten or 12 tons of water would lower the keel at least 6–8 in.

Our worst bridge was at Attercliffe, near Sheffield. Sometimes we had to use crowbars to force the keel under, and when we finally got through, Dad had to steer the keel and pump out the water while Mother and I pulled by man-line.

Quite close to this bridge the canal passed over a main road, and I used to think it was wonderful to see the traffic going underneath us. It was a novelty for us to be watching, for whenever we had to go through a lock or under a bridge there were always spectators. 'Gawpers' my mother used to call them.

There were other causes of delay: a damaged lock could detain us for a whole day, and rain, too, could cause us trouble. If it had rained heavily around Sheffield, the Don would rise and there would be such a strong current that we needed two horses instead of one, which added to the expense of the trip. The Don was not tidal in these parts and had only an ebb running down from Sheffield. Sometimes we would have to stop at Doncaster, where we left the canal and entered the Don, because the hauling banks were under water. This extra water was called fresh, and we could be 'freshbound' for anything from a day to a week, waiting until the water went down. Sometimes the fresh would cause the river to silt up, and we would have to wait until the Canal Company dredger cleared a channel. This often happened at Jordan Pond where the river joins the canal at Tinsley. Instead of waiting for the dredger there, we would sometimes put our four or five horses together and by using the windlass and attaching the rope to something solid on the bank we would scour our way through the mud with the first keel so that the others could follow. There could be a dozen keels held up in this way, and then there would be a mad rush to get to Sheffield first, seize a berth and discharge. It was first come first served, and not only fair means were used. There was sometimes fighting between keelmen sneaking turns,

4a. The fore end of a wooden keel

4b. Detail of the centrepiece
decorated with gold leaf

5. The *Faith* moored in Thorne 'rack'

6. The wooden swing bridge at Stainforth

and once one of them set off at night from the locks in his stocking feet. There was a big strike on at the collieries at that time and loads were scarce, so the 'stocking feet' keelman got the only load that week. The rest of the keels had to travel light.

Small things wasted our time too. For instance, we had to unship and leave parts of the keel's tackle at various places on the route, and of course pick them up and re-assemble them on the return journey.

At Thorne we left the leeboards, because they were a nuisance, as the canal was very narrow, and without them we had 6 in extra clearance. We left the anchors there too, as they were no use except in the Humber. The lock-keeper looked after them for the fee of 1s. Our voyage continued from Stainforth to Bramwith, where we left the coggy boat and the towrope for 6d. The lock-keeper even bailed the boat out for that.

From Bramwith we followed the canal to Kirk Sandall and Doncaster, and from there the route was very complicated and time-consuming, alternating as it did between river and canal several times. We went out of the canal into the Don at Doncaster, through Hexthorpe Flats and Warmsworth Cliffs to Sprotborough Lock, where we left the Don and entered a short stretch of canal. But it was back into the Don at Conisborough Lock and on to Denaby, where we came out of the river and into the canal to Mexborough. Here we unshipped the mast and sails and left them in the lock-keeper's care for 1s. We could never sail on this stretch anyway.

The canal took us on to Swinton and Kilnhurst, where the Kilnhurst Flood Lock took us back into the river Don to Aldwarke. Another lock there took us back into the canal to Eastwood and Rotherham, where we returned to the Don as far as Ickles Lock. Then it was back to the canal through Holmes Lock and Jordan Lock.

The Don took us on to Tinsley four locks, and then it was canal again to the other eight locks at Tinsley, and that lovely top level which took us at last to Attercliffe and Sheffield, where our voyage ended and so did the canal.

It was there that we had to pay our canal dues, for the canal was financed by dues which were so much per ton of cargo. There was a fixed due for each section of canal, and at Thorne and Mexborough the lock-keepers had to sign a bill of lading for us.

We took these bills into the canal offices at Sheffield, but they were paid by the people who bought the cargo, and not by us.

We had to pay the incidental expenses of the voyage. The main ones were 10s for the steam-tug and 32s for horse marines, and the lesser ones were 1s for leaving the leeboards, 6d for the boat, 1s for the mast and sails, and about 2s 6d in tips for unloading at Sheffield.

The price for taking grain from Hull to Sheffield was 2s 6d per ton, which made a freight of £11 5s. We went 'thirds' with this. A third had to be given to the owner of the keel, which left us with £7 10s, and after deducting £2 17s for expenses we were left with £4 13s unless the captain had to pay 8s for a 'purchase man' from Hull to Keadby (an extra man being called a 'purchase man').

From the age of twelve I saved my father that expense, and before I was that age my mother and I together did the job. After we had bought clothes and paid the rent of the house in Thorne there was little left over for food, and as we all lived in the open air we all had good appetites. Still, £1 a week was a good wage in those times when farm labourers had only about 15s 6d, but we had to work for it.

The return load of coal fetched a little less, about 1s 10d a ton, with 21 cwt to the ton from our collieries, half a ton of which was given to us for our own use. As the depth of canal regulated the amount of cargo we carried, we usually managed 90 tons to Sheffield, and 110 tons of coal back to Hull. Our price then was about £10 1s 8d which left us with only £3 7s 2½d.

Money was always scarce when I was a lad, as sailing, the cheapest way of travelling, was beginning to die out. Towing by steam-tug and horses, we could do the voyage from Hull to Thorne in one day, but it took three by sail. We could do the entire journey in four to four and a half days if everything went according to plan. Our times were: Hull to Thorne on the first day; Thorne to Mexborough on the second; Mexborough to Sheffield on the third. That left us a day or a day and a half for loading, unloading, and unforeseen delays. Of course, if the journey took longer, it simply meant that our money had to go further.

Once and once only a keel did the journey in an incredible fifteen hours. The manager of Rank's in Hull gave 60 tons of flour to Fred Bisby of Thorne and 60 tons to the railway just to see which could get to Sheffield first. Fred only had his wife with him but they did it in fifteen hours. They set off at 5 p.m. and worked all night. There was no sleep for either of them.

Although our usual voyage was along the Sheffield and South Yorkshire canals to Doncaster, Swinton, Mexborough, Rotherham, Tinsley and Sheffield, we did not always call at the same collieries on the way back. We collected loads from Dalton Main, or Roundwood as we called it because they only used round pit-props, Kilnhurst or Denaby or Cadeby, and sometimes, using a branch canal at Swinton, we went to the Elsecar and Barnsley collieries.

The route up the Humber and then the Ouse to Goole, York and Selby was one we seldom took. It was called the West Country route, but we did sometimes use part of it, going via Goole up the Aire and Calder Canal to cut through a branch canal to Bramwith, where we rejoined our own Sheffield and South Yorkshire route. I never knew much about the Aire and Calder Canal, except that it went to Knottingley and Leeds. It has special boats, small and narrow craft called flyboats, working it.

These flyboats were smaller than keels but larger than narrow boats and had their own style of building with long narrow plates and cup-head riveting. There were different types, long ones and short ones. The short ones took general cargo via the Humber, the Ouse and the Aire and Calder Canal from Goole to Huddersfield, Halifax and Bingley and other canals and rivers in that area. The long ones went to the Leeds and Liverpool canals. The families lived aboard them.

They all loaded up outside the docks in Humber dock basin and were towed up the Humber by tug and up the river Ouse by horse marine as they had no sails.

Sometimes we took a load from Goole to Hull, but as we could not use the sail on the Ouse, it was not an economical run.

Goole was a very busy port, but because it was a long way from the sea the size of ships using its docks was limited to about 1,500 tons. A lot of coal was loaded there for regular trade to the electric power stations at Ipswich and Battersea, and they also loaded coal, coke and general cargo for the Continent.

We never went further up the river Hull than Stoneferry, although some keels did. Some even went to Driffield on the canal, or to Beverley on Beverley Beck. Other keels used the canal to Market Weighton via Newport, and others went to the brick-yards at Broomfleet, but we stuck to the Sheffield and South Yorkshire run. We did once go further up the Trent to Torksey, but had to stop there as the keel was too big to go into the canals, and we had to rig up a temporary derrick and discharge our cargo of wheat into narrow boats.

I did hear of one keel called the *Minnie*, captained by a man called Cook, which once took coal to Bridlington harbour. It was house coal and was of course much cheaper for people to buy than coal transported by rail. The *Minnie* had a sloop rig, that is, her sail was fore and aft instead of square, and as that was her only power, Mr Cook had to pick his weather since keels were not designed for coastal trade. Of course she was never out of sight of land from leaving the Humber to getting to Bridlington, but there was no shelter from the sea after leaving the Humber. If a keel was caught in a squall she just had to drop anchor (we called it letting down the mud hook), take down the sail and ride it out. Strong winds and gales from the north, north-east and north-west blew straight on to that coastline, and they were usually very cold.

I never knew whether this was an isolated adventure, as keel-men rarely kept written records. So few knew how to read and write. One who could was Ernest Downing of Stainforth. He was known as the 'keelman's lawyer', and often helped keelmen in their disputes with carrying agents, and wrote letters for them when they were in trouble.

I did hear of another keelman called Wright, who used his square-rigged keel to take coal to Withernsea on the east coast. He had to be even more careful of the weather, as there was no harbour at Withernsea where he could take shelter. He had to discharge into carts drawn up on the beach. This trade did not continue long as the risks were too great. If his keel had been caught in a northerly gale, she would have been broken up in no time by being pounded on the beach, and because the wind was always blowing on to that coast she would not have been able to sail off and ride it out.

It was a great adventure to go on these voyages by sea, but there were always two experienced rivermen on board, the captain and his mate. They had to be experienced, for they had no channel markings and no navigation aids, not even a compass. They just stayed in sight of land, watched out for sandbanks, and kept on sounding for depth.

Sounding really needed three men: one to scull the coggy boat, one to swing the lead-line, and one to note down the details of the bottom of the channel and its depth. The lead-line was a lead weight 9–12 in in length, hollowed out at the bottom and filled with tallow so that particles of sand, mud or rock could attach themselves. If the bottom was rock we were in real trouble, for we could so easily hole the keel and sink.

The lead itself had a ring at the top with a sounding rope attached, and the rope had coloured pieces of strong tape marking each fathom so that we could find the depth of the water at the same time. A friend has told me that on the Bayeux Tapestry, where the Norman ships are shown coming in to land, a sailor can be seen using a lead-line exactly like the one I used to swing in the Humber as a boy.

Another captain, Mizpah Holt, showed even more initiative. He rigged his keel, the *Drucilla*, with a sloop rig and ventured as far along the coast as Louth in Lincolnshire. He had a relative in the coal business in Louth so decided to try to deliver coal there. First he took general cargo to Sheffield or Rotherham for 'livering' (we were always either 'loading' or 'livering') and then went up a branch canal from Swinton to Barnsley to collect his coal from Manvers Main colliery. He could only carry 70 tons because the *Drucilla* was a smaller keel than ours. We couldn't get to Manvers Main.

From Manvers Main he went to sea the usual way, through Keadby Locks, along the Trent to the Humber. Once at sea there was nothing to guide him as there were no channels marked on the Lincolnshire coast. He had to take a bearing from Spurn Lighthouse to a point on the coastline and then find a channel. This was quite difficult as there are sandbanks all along the coast of Lincolnshire and the entrance to Tetney Haven which led into Tetney Lock and the Louth Canal was particularly difficult to find. Once or twice he went past it and had to turn back. This was annoying as it often caused the keel to be left at sea a long time, perhaps waiting for the next tide. It was dangerous, too, as rough weather could badly damage a keel.

Occasionally, when cargoes were hard to get, we would take the place of lighters, or floating warehouses. Lighters are similar to keels, but they have no gear and no one lives on them. We would load a cargo of linseed, cotton seed, palm kernels, copra, rape seed or locust seed, and lay in the dock until it was wanted at one of the mills in the river Hull. We were paid so much a ton to take the seed from the dock to the mills, and after four days in the dock we were charged so much a day demurrage, which was like paying rent.

There are still a lot of lighters in Hull. Lightermen go to work in the morning, load a lighter, and if the tides are suitable, take it by tug into the river Hull to the mills and discharge. This might mean working until ten or eleven at night. Sometimes they have to take a lighter round at two or three o'clock in the morning, depending on the tides, discharge the cargo and then take the boat back into the dock—a very tiring job.

2 *Waterway hazards*

I have had some good times on the Humber, the Trent, the Ouse, the Don and the Hull, but also some bad ones especially on the Humber, which can change from a smooth river to a very rough one in the space of an hour or less. I enjoyed sailing the Humber in good summer weather, but in bad times it was a constant fight with the tides and the sandbanks, and one which we did not always win.

The channel in the Humber was very narrow in some places in comparison with the width of the river and as it was always moving, soundings had to be taken regularly and the passage marked by lightships and gas buoys, which had bells rung by steel rods suspended from the light tower. The motion of the buoys caused the rods to swing and hit the bell, which served as a warning in fog. On top of the tower was a light which flashed at regular intervals, and was powered by gas stored in the cylinders and automatically released. These cylinders were replenished and examined regularly by a Humber Conservancy tender. Some of the buoys were painted red with red flashing lights, and some black with white flashing lights, the colour telling the river pilots on which side of the buoy they should go.

When you entered the Humber from the sea the first lightship was the Bull Light, then the Spurn Light, both manned by a crew. There were buoys and floats right up to Whitton Sands, just north of Read's Island. These were very dangerous sandbanks, always on the move, and they had three manned lightships, the Lower, Middle and Upper Whitton lightships. There were lighthouses on land as well, one of them at Paull.

There was another sandbank off Grimsby, a third off Paull and a fourth running up the middle of the river to a point just outside Barton. One sandbank called Holme Sand has disappeared since my days on the river.

The Middle Sand off Hull bares at spring tides, and you can walk on it, as I have done many times and picked up coal for the fire.

There were other channels in the river that could be used to advantage by small craft and many captains of keels made the most of them as they knew the river very well indeed.

Once, when Dad and I set off from Hull to sail an empty keel to Keadby for a cargo of coal, we had left Humber Dock, and got beyond St. Andrew's Dock when Dad decided that as the keel was light we could go over the sandbank that lies off Hessle. We were sailing along well when we struck the sand where we were stuck for the best part of a day. I remember how the edge of the bank looked as if it had been cut off with a shovel. It was dead straight. We were not in any real danger as the weather was clear, but time was money to us and that day's delay could have lost us the cargo of coal. As it was we just had to wait on the sandbank for the tide to lift us off.

Dad had misjudged after a lifetime on the river, and rivermen are still misjudging. It was only in the late 1960s that a riverman mistook the amount of water in the river just like Dad. He had an oil-tank barge, and was cutting three or four miles off his journey by going across instead of along the channel. He was travelling light, and thought he could do it, but he touched bottom and the barge turned over. He and his partner were saved, but his little girl, taken for the first time as a treat, was not.

Another time, sailing from Keadby to Hull, it suddenly became so foggy that we had to stop and drop anchor. I had to sit in the forecastle with the fogbell which we hung in the hatchway, and I had to ring it every thirty seconds. There was no going to sleep, and the fog lasted all night. I was only ten at the time and very frightened. We also had to hang up a riding light at the forestay of the mast and make sure it did not go out. Luckily it was not cold. Although we were anchored, Dad still had to steer the keel for two hours until the tide eased, for it was so strong that if it had caught us broadside on we should have been pulled under and flooded. Fog was a very bad thing on the river, for though there were the foghorns and lightships, it was still very difficult to judge distances especially by sound. It was always better to drop anchor and wait for clear weather.

Tides were often very fierce. Even on a normal trip it was a full-time job attending to the sails and steering in the river, and we often had no food or drink for six or seven hours. It was not possible to stop when the tides were averaging between 5 and 7 knots, depending on whether they were spring or neap tides, for they were very powerful, and sometimes there was what we called an 'overflow'. That meant that they were higher and faster than shown in the tidetables, and we had to keep a sharp watch as they could easily put the keel in a dangerous position. For instance, the captain might not estimate the room correctly, and would get pushed on to a sandbank or on to one of the stone heaps piled on the river banks to break the tides and to prevent the banks from being washed away. A normal tide ran on an average of about five hours and the ebb about seven. At Hull the rise and fall varied between eighteen and twenty-two feet.

Once, on our way to Grimsby by sail, we were nearly blown out to sea, having missed the entry to Royal Dock. Luckily a tug picked us up and took us back. On another occasion we left St. Andrew's Dock with a light, or empty keel. The wind was against us so we could not sail and the alternative was to haul by hand. I got on to the bank and began to pull with the seal, Mother steered, and Dad pushed with a boat-hook until we reached River-side Quay. Once alongside the quay, hauling by hand from the bank was impossible because ships from the Continent were discharging fruit and vegetables the full length of the dock. There was no tug available to move us. So I had to get into our coggy boat and scull with a single oar to take a light line, called a warping line, to the boltheads, which held the wooden piles of the quay. It was no easy task for a ten year old. I waved to Dad to heave away and got my thumb fast in the line. I had to wait until the keel caught up with me before I could get it out, by which time it was as flat as a piece of paper. It still aches when I think about it!

In a gale the Humber looked grey and savage, and life on the keel was most uncomfortable. We rolled and pitched among waves that washed right over us. It seemed as if a storm trapped in that

41

narrow estuary grew fiercer and fiercer because it could not get out, and it thrashed away until all its power and bad temper were spent. We called rough waves 'Hessle whelps' near Hessle, and 'Barton bulldogs' near Barton.

Storms even in the canal could be frightening. We were once sailing in squally weather to Keadby from Thorne with a load of coal for the trawlers in Hull when a thunderstorm struck us and our mast broke off and fell across the canal. The top of the mast hit the hauling bank and snapped off so the main part of the mast and the sails were in the water. It was a good job nothing was near us as we blocked the canal for a long time.

We moved to the bank and Mother and brother Bill set off to walk to Crowle Station not far away, to catch a train to Thorne. They took the measurements of the mast with them so that they could inform the owner and order a new mast.

Meanwhile we were stuck. Dad and I started to pull the mast and sails out of the canal and it was a tough job. First we tried to get the sail off the mast and on to the keel's sidedeck so that the water could drain away but it was heavy work as wet sailcloth stiffens and is very bad to handle. It skins your finger-ends if you're not careful.

Then we had to get the unbroken sail yard-arm off the mast: a real test of strength for Dad and me but we managed it although I was only 4 ft 6 in. All the rigging had to be rescued, too—the halyards, hoisting gear and mast and shrouds—and it all had to be pulled on board by hand as our only means of lifting by winch was by using the mast itself, and that was in the canal.

When the mast was finally stripped it was in three pieces. The bottom was in the lutchet; the middle, about 25 ft, was in the canal; and the top was on the bank. The bottom and top were easy to retrieve but the 25 ft piece—8–9 in in diameter—was more difficult.

We had a bit of scheming to do. Dad decided that the only chance we had was to put two ropes across the keel's hatch, loop them under the mast, one at each end, and then pull the ropes over the mast and on to the far side of the keel. We then rolled the mast up between the ropes, but it was so heavy that we had to work together doing a little bit at one side and then a little bit at the other. We were absolutely tired out when we did get it on board and it was almost dark so we had to pull the keel by hand to Crowle Wharf to wait for Mother and Bill.

That night Dad worked out how we could fix the mast temporarily. We needed it for sailing and for discharging the coal in Hull. So we started the next morning. Dad shaped the middle section of the mast the best he could to fit in the lutchet; then we put up the rigging. It didn't look too bad. We hauled by hand to Keadby and then sailed successfully with our makeshift mast to Hull.

The accident had cost us a full day's delay and a lot of hard work. Keelmen had to be handy in all sorts of ways because accidents like these invariably happened when no one was near. If other keels had been at hand, all the men would have lent a hand. Although keelmen competed keenly for cargoes, in cases like this they all helped each other.

Nearly every winter the land was flooded between Stainforth and Bramwith and we had to steer by the trees and the field hedges because the canal banks were under water, and in cold weather I have seen the Humber full of floating ice from bank to bank. Once, near Paull I saw blocks 8–10 ft high washed on to the land, but I have never seen the Humber frozen even in keenest winter.

There were always gulls flying about, especially near the fish docks where there was plenty for them to eat and there were curlews and ducks all the year round in the upper reaches. Geese came in season and it was a grand sight to see them migrating hundreds at a time and always in strict formation. There was even an odd swan or two but they didn't swim on the Humber as it was too rough and they didn't like the shipping. At busy times there could be as many as twenty ships and trawlers on the move, the big ones giving their deep-throated three hoots for pilots. But the swans flew over sometimes and settled on the brickponds at each side of the river.

On spring tides in the Trent there is a bore called the Aegir (or Eagre). I have heard tell that this is the Danish word for the god of the water, and that whenever the eagre appeared the god was angry. But it was really caused by the incoming tide rushing over the ebb, and we had to be sure not to be caught broadside by it. On neap tides the ebb ceases before the tide meets it, so there is no bore.

When the bore did come it was usually in the early morning or evening and if we were near Keadby jetty we always made fast, facing the direction it would come. Cabin hatches were closed fore and aft in case water came over the top but we stayed on deck so that we could patch up any covers that got loose. We had to work quickly or the cargo would have been damaged. This often entailed getting nice and wet with no means of getting dry again until we were out of the rough weather.

You could hear it a mile away, roaring along the river banks. It looked like a huge wave, varying from six, to eight feet in height and coming down the river with as many as six rollers, which we called whelps, behind it. When it hit us, the keel seemed to rise three feet forward and yet the water was six feet lower aft. It was a funny sensation and when the bore had passed the water in the river had risen by four or five feet. Of course where the Trent was narrower, the wave was higher.

My father sometimes talked about the river Trent freezing and a horse and cart trotting across the ice, and I can remember when the canal was frozen solid and my father skated the eleven miles from Keadby to Thorne. The Canal Company made an ice-breaker and even that got frozen in. The usual method of ice-breaking was to have six men in a boat rocking away furiously while a horse hauled them from the bank. If this failed everything had to stop. We had iron plates to hang in front of the keel to prevent ice cutting into the wood.

On a good summer's day it was pleasant sailing on the rivers although you had to be prepared for anything and it could become rough in a very short time. Winter or summer I always treated the river with the greatest respect; to do otherwise was foolish.

From a hill at the Trent end of the river you could see almost to Hull and a large part of the flat lands of Yorkshire and Lincolnshire. You got a wonderful view too of the three rivers: the Trent, the Ouse and the Humber.

But even in summer the water in the Humber looked grey and muddy. The scent of the air was a mixture of salt, sea and mud. I liked the smell of the water at night and it was a grand sight approaching Hull as all the docks were lit up and the lamps in the city shone like fairy lights. They made a glow in the sky especially if the clouds were low, and we could also see the lights of Hessle, and on the other side of the river Barton and New Holland Pier twinkled away. It really looked well. Sometimes we could even see the red glow in the sky from Scunthorpe as they tipped the molten slag at the steel works over the hills on the Lincolnshire side.

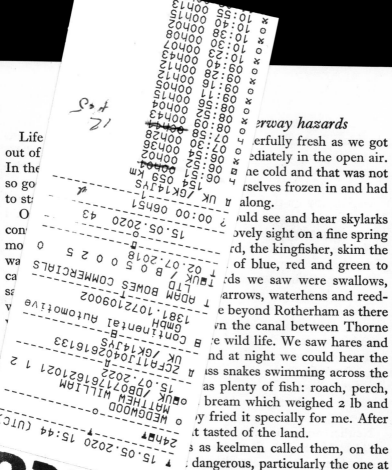

Life ...erfully fresh as we got
out of ...ediately in the open air.
In the ...he cold and that was not
so go... ...rselves frozen in and had
to st... ...along.

O... ...uld see and hear skylarks
con... ...ovely sight on a fine spring
mo... ...rd, the kingfisher, skim the
wa... ... of blue, red and green to
ca... ...rds we saw were swallows,
sa... ...arrows, waterhens and reed-
v... ...e beyond Rotherham as there
... ...n the canal between Thorne
... ...e wild life. We saw hares and
... ...nd at night we could hear the
... ...ss snakes swimming across the
... ...as plenty of fish: roach, perch,
... ...bream which weighed 2 lb and
... ...y fried it specially for me. After
... ...t tasted of the land.

...s as keelmen called them, on the
... ...dangerous, particularly the one at
... ...joins the canal at a right angle and
... ...he lock gates leading into the canal.
... ...ght over this one, as after heavy rain
... ...r the top could be anything from two
... ...ebb flowing it was easy to be swept
... ...river.

...sion when we were in Sheffield all the
k... ...and lock... ...were saying as we passed, 'Hello, Young
Jim! Is it your secon... ...ne on earth?' This was because a story
had passed all the way up river to Sheffield that my father had
been knocked overboard and drowned at Hull. There were many
such tragedies. I have seen them happen in the fish dock, and in
broad daylight.

Once a man fell in at the bridge-way across the fish dock
extension. Between it and the fish dock was a swing bridge which
at night was left open to dock traffic. A chain was put across the
pedestrian road, but I suppose the man tripped over this and fell
into the dock. A policeman heard a shout, saw a cap floating on

the water and called for help. They grappled for him, and I saw him pulled up in the light of the gaslamps. His mouth and his eyes were wide open, and the grappling iron was stuck in his waistcoat. I shall never forget that. I can see him now.

At Keadby on the canal a boy of my age, about ten, who had been sailing a coggy boat, was drowned when it turned over. I had to help grapple for him. We put a grapple hook on a line and pulled backwards and forwards across the canal from each bank. He came up at my end, and I dropped the line and bolted.

A grappling-iron was a three-pronged hook on the end of a rope, and it had to be pulled back and forth either by boat or from the dockside. It was of no use in a tideway, but in still water it hooked into the clothes of the drowned person. If the body had not been found it would have floated to the surface in nine days, unless it had stuck fast to something in the water, in which case a diver had to go down for it.

On two different occasions we saw bodies floating in the Humber when we were being towed by steam-tug, but we could do nothing except report them as soon as we reached land.

Neither my father nor my grandfather could swim. No more could I. Most of the keelmen I knew couldn't either, except my Uncle Joe. I am not exactly afraid of water, but I have a great respect for it especially when it is combined with a strong wind. I always said that if there was more than would fill a bath there was too much.

I have had my share of falling in. We were once waiting to load coal at Denaby where the coal hoist is in the middle of the river. The hatchboards had been taken off the hold and put at the ends of the keel, and I was struggling with the long narrow board called the mastboard which covered the mast way, when my feet shot from under me, and mastboard and I began to slip into the river. I let go of the mastboard and just managed to grab a lashing which held the man-rope in place. I was safe, if wet, and shouted my head off for Dad to come while I hung on with one hand. He pulled me out eventually and I got a good talking to for losing that mastboard. I was only eleven and thought myself hard done by. I had grazed my arm and it was painful but we had to take on the coal or miss our turn to load so there was no rest for me. We loaded, covered up, washed down and set off. Dad was still angry about losing the mastboard but when we reached Conis-

46

borough Lock there it was. It had floated down the river and the lock-keeper had picked it out. Dad was happy again but I had a bad arm which was sore for several days. That was the only time I had ever been in danger of drowning from the keel although I have fallen in both the canal and the large drains at Keadby while fishing from the banks.

I have often thought of all the risks we took, jumping off walls on to the keels when they were moving, especially at the locks when a mistimed jump would have meant falling and being crushed between the lockside and the boat. But we were all sure-footed and careful never to wear hob-nailed boots or clogs with irons. They would have been too slippery and dangerous.

Duckings were not always tragic. My grandad, Lemon Bill, once left Uncle Joe alone on board the keel one weekend while he went home to Thorne.

Now Uncle Joe liked to have a drink, and when Grandad returned to the keel on Monday morning, he found men grappling in Albert Dock. He was shocked to hear that they were grappling for Uncle Joe, and even more shocked to hear that it was not unknown for Joe to come back drunk at weekends. Since the men had heard a splash the night before, and Joe was not aboard the next morning, they feared the worst. Grandad took a hand in the grappling, and had not been at it long when he felt a hand on his shoulder, and heard a voice say, 'Who've you lost?' 'You, you old boozer!' roared Grandad, for of course it was Uncle Joe. He was never allowed to forget either the trouble he'd caused, or the night out he'd had.

People were always falling in somewhere. Especially accident-prone were wives new to the canals. I'm sure Catherine Ackroyd won't mind me telling a few of her adventures aboard the *Lily* and the *Crane*.

She came from Salthouse Lane, near the High Street in Hull, and married a keelman from Thorne. It was on her first voyage, when they were towing up the river, that her husband asked her to drop a fender over the side. Naturally she ran to the fire in the cabin for the only fender she knew—but she managed to live that down. Looking back to her keel days, and she was eighty-six when telling these stories, she seems to have spent most of her time in and out of the canal.

The first fright she had was when she was sitting on the hatchway

47

as the keel went under a low bridge, and she was knocked senseless into the water. Her husband fished her out.

Then she fell into the cut because she took the high toll bar instead of the low toll bar. Rescued that time by two young men, she was recognized and returned to her own keel, but she had been badly scared. It wasn't funny to fall in, no matter how ridiculous it looked.

She has one lovely story about a nameless keelman who was taking two women of the town to his keel in Alexandra Dock. He handed them into his coggy boat to row them across, and half-way there it sprang a leak and began to sink. The women began to scream and shout, floundering in the water, and it was Mrs Ackroyd's husband who went to their rescue, pulling them out and very nearly pushing them in again when he discovered who they were. 'Wish I'd left them in the dock!' he said to her. 'They were no good.'

Alexandra Dock was always known as 'Soakem' to keelmen, because the entrance was so rough, and a gale could cause havoc inside the dock.

In severe gales all river traffic came to a standstill, as it was dangerous to dock a heavy vessel in the constricted space of a dock, since they could do great damage to locks and jetties. We were once in the dock when a three-masted sailing-ship broke loose in a strong wind and sank some lighters, but by good luck missed us. It was rumoured that there were so many claims for damages, true and false, that the captain committed suicide.

Not long afterwards a steamship, moored stern on, broke adrift and my father and two other keelmen managed to catch a rope from it and helped the crew to get it back to its moorings. The captain, who was a German, came over to our keel next morning to thank my father and had a cup of tea with us in the cabin, which he was surprised to find so comfortable. I don't know what he expected! He gave my brother and me sixpence each. We were rich! He also gave my father some money to share with the other keelmen, so Dad had a good day as well.

It was in this same dock that we once had to get up at two o'clock in the morning to move the keel for a ship to berth. There was a blizzard blowing. Mother and I had to heave the keel on the warping-line while Dad pushed with a boat-hook. I don't think I have ever been so cold before or since. The handlings we

7.   The double locks at Keadby

8.   The Aegir on the Trent

9. The tugs *Welshman* and *Irishman*

10. The bridgeman's lobby at Toll Bar Bridge, Thorne

used for heaving were made of iron and stuck to our hands with the frost. All my mother's finger-ends cracked open, and so did two of mine. I think that was when I made up my mind that being a keelman was not for me.

Once, one of the large merchant ships arrived at Hull in a very strong gale of wind and it took four tugs, instead of the usual two, to get her to her berth in Alexandra Dock. We were in the same dock on our keel at the time, and on the alert in case she broke away from the tugs. If she had, she would have crushed our keel to matchwood, and we would have had to jump on the land smartish. It was a bitterly cold day, and it took them almost two hours to get her to the berth and made secure, an operation which normally took half an hour. The wind was south-west and blowing right on the lock, and when the gates were closed the waves were going right over the top of everything. The Dockmaster's office was flooded, and the Customs and the Dock-gatemen's lobby. Water was even washing over the roads and running into the docks. This was another event which made me decide not to be a keelman.

But it was in the docks that I enjoyed myself most. I loved to watch all the ships. They were all different. In the fish docks I watched the sea-going trawlers belonging to Sir Christopher Pickering who was well known in West Hull, where a park, a maritime museum and a church bear his name. His trawlers were of sturdy construction and were good sea boats. They landed very good-quality fish, usually in the early hours, two or three in the morning, and it was sold to the fish merchants after seven o'clock. These trawlers had only from twenty-four to thirty-six hours in dock, then they were off to sea again.

My father brought them coal from the South Yorkshire collieries in the *Mary Ward* for they were steam-trawlers, called 'fleeters' or 'boxmen', and stayed out at sea for six weeks at a time and transferred their catch into 'carriers' or 'cutters', which took it straight to Billingsgate. The *Northern Hill* was one of these. My Uncle Joe went to sea on her. He said they worked twenty-four and a quarter hours a day, and the rest of the time was your own. His arms were covered in tiny boils called sea-boils caused by gutting fish.

When these trawlers were setting out, they put their own meat and vegetables on top of the ice which they took to keep the fish fresh. When they had used all the ice they put the rest of the meat into brine. This was called 'salt tack', and any of it left at the end of the voyage was thrown away as it was unwise to have any food over when the ship's husband came on board. He worked for the ship's owners, and his job was to see that the trawlers were provisioned for each trip. If there had been a scrap too much he would have cut down the rations for the next trip, and there was usually little enough. Most trawlermen took food of their own to vary and eke out the diet. They more often ran out of stock than had any left.

All trawlers used St. Andrew's Dock, where there were fish-landing quays at one side and ice-houses and coal-hoists at the other. They unloaded their fish at one side and went across the other to load ice and provisions for their next trip. Near the ice-houses, where ice was made, were fish-manure works and cod farms where cod fish was salted and dried for export. This work was all done by women who walked down to the fish docks early in the morning, their clogs rattling on the granite brick roads, singing at the tops of their voices. The din was terrific—you could hear them half a mile away.

I used to watch the Humber sloops which took goods across the river to Barton and New Holland. On market days in Hull, Tuesdays and Fridays, they would lie inside Corporation Pier at the horse wash, where horses and carts went down to the river so that the horses could paddle in the water and revive their feet. The sloops unloaded farm produce from Lincolnshire, and loaded animal feeding stuffs from the mills at Hull, and any general cargo such as furniture and farm implements. It was even possible to send small parcels aboard them and sometimes they took stones to mend the river banks. They were good sailing craft, captained mostly by their owners and were for hire for almost any job. They had a type of sail known as a Gaff and Boom which was not suitable for use in narrow waterways, but which was easier to handle than our square sails.

A smaller type of sloop of wooden construction was used in the Humber to get sand for ballast in empty ocean-going ships. They would go down the river below Paull and anchor on the Holme Sand to wait until the tide left them dry on the sandbank. Then the crew of two would get on to the sand, which was quite firm, and with steel-tipped shovels dig up the sand and throw it into the open hold. They had no hatches. It was very hard work, since they had to load 40 or 50 tons in five or six hours before the tide came back and floated them off. They sailed back to Hull and sold the sand to any ships requiring ballast.

When ships became double-bottomed and used water ballast, their work was finished. I last saw sand sloops at work during the First World War when they brought sand for filling sandbags to protect buildings against the bombs dropped by the zeppelins.

I remember four paddle-tugs, the *United*, the *Lady Butte*, the *Hutton* and the *Powerful*, owned by William Gray & Co., the largest tug-owners in Hull, or by the Stephen Gray Co. They must have been built in the late 1800s as they were old when I knew them in 1908. They went out almost to the mouth of the river and picked up ships as they entered the Humber, then agreed to dock them for a certain price, which included undocking as well. They often towed a small rowing boat with them, the owner of which would agree to take the ropes to the quay and help to fasten, and when the time came, to unfasten the ship.

They were also used for towing small barges from Hull to Goole but were not very handy in use, as in most of them the paddles could not be worked separately and this made them awkward to turn round. They towed a lot of narrow boats or flyboats, which had to be towed all the time because they had no sailing gear. They could work in any of the docks in Hull except St. Andrew's. The trawlers and herring drifters were small enough to manœuvre themselves in and out of dock without the help of tugs.

Most of the tugs carried a pump and hose for fire-fighting and they were often in use. Some of them also had large pumps for salvage work, particularly the later steel-built ones.

The *United* had a single engine which meant both her paddle wheels worked together. This made her awkward to turn especially in a confined space. She was all right when towing and had a fair amount of pulling power.

Crews had to be on duty at tide times, twice every twenty-four hours, and sometimes in between tides to tow ships from the discharging berths for refuelling. Usually they had a crew of four: the captain, the engineer who stoked his own boiler, a deckhand to attend to the ropes, and a cabin boy for making tea and helping with the ropes when towing was over. The engineer would bank up the boiler fires before he left, but would have to be back on board before the others to get up steam.

Since tides worked round the clock, the men might be on duty at 3 p.m. and 3.40 a.m. the next day. On average, each tide was forty minutes later than the last, and it would be about a fortnight before the same tide came round again, so the men were on duty four, five or even six hours at each tide, at different times of day or night. It was not much of a life socially, either for them or their families, but there always seemed to be plenty of men for the job. The captain was paid a wage and a share of the tug's earnings called poundage.

The Wilson Line had a large number of merchant ships, and kept four tugs to do their own towing instead of hiring them. They had the *Presto*, a twin-funnel paddle-tug, and the *Plato*, the *Jumbo* and the *Varro*, which were single-screw propeller tugs. The *Plato* and the *Jumbo* were iron, but the *Varro* was steel.

The *Presto*, built in the late 1800s had twin engines which enabled her to turn quickly, as by going ahead with one paddle and astern with the other she could turn completely round without moving either forwards or backwards. This was a great improvement on the fixed paddles.

The tug I liked best was the *Varro*. I used to think she was a wonderful boat, and I had her painted on our cabin hatch in no time. The captain saw me painting her as she was lying against us and when he had to take her out towing he promised to bring her back to berth against us so that I could have my model until the next tide. He looked at my painting every time he could manage it, and then one day he took me aboard and let me have a real look round. I was delighted! I would have given him the cabin hatch if he had asked for it.

The *Varro* was the forerunner of modern tugs and the pride of Hull in her day. She had good lines, and the bulwarks were laid inboard, giving a much better appearance, and helping to reduce damage to them. The engine room casing and wheelhouse were neater too, and she had a triple expansion engine which meant that the steam was used three times. It went from the boiler to the high-pressure cylinder, through valves to the medium-pressure cylinder, and then through more valves into the low-pressure cylinder, then to the condenser where it was cooled and then used again. Once the engine was started, there was nothing to do except alter speed or reverse, as the captain required, and keep everything well oiled. It was a dream of a boat!

There was always one of these tugs on duty for moving ships in the docks. I do not know what the pay was, but it must have been satisfactory, as they were never short of crews. The tug wore the Wilson Line colours: red funnels with green hulls. They were always busy and known all over the Humber.

William Gray also owned a boat called the *Frenchman*. She doubled as a tug in winter, working the Hull docks, but in summer she ran pleasure trips from Bridlington harbour, which was probably why she did not wear the company's colours. She had a yellow funnel and a grey hull.

She was about the last of the paddle-tugs in Hull. Passengers could sit on the bridge deck or on the lower deck, and seats were placed around the inside of the bulwarks. She had a licensed bar in the saloon, which was forward, and the crew lived aft.

Sometimes she took in coal from the fish quay. It was brought by lorry in bags, just as it was delivered to houses, and emptied down a chute into the bunkers below deck.

The crew wore white caps and navy blue jerseys and trousers. She stopped her towing jobs about three weeks before going to Bridlington to be repainted. She looked quite well when ready to go. They steamed round Flamborough Head, and sometimes north to Scarborough, or south to Hornsea.

These pleasure trips were taken over by the single-screw propeller tug, the *Yorkshireman*, after the *Frenchman* finished. She ended her days as a coal boat in the river Hull. Tugs too small for the coal-hoists would go to her for bunker coal. She had her engines and boiler taken out to provide more room, then she was towed across the Humber to New Holland, loaded with coal and towed back to lie just inside the river Hull.

Other ships that fascinated me were the immigrant ships from the Balkans that moored near us in the corner of the Albert Dock, where we moored when we were waiting for a cargo so that we were out of the way of the normal river traffic. They probably moored there for the same reason, except that they were waiting for other ships to take their living cargo to America.

These immigrants were Russian Jews, and they were not allowed off the dock during their stay of one or two days, but they were permitted to come off their ship in the evening after the

53

dockers had finished work. It was then that I watched them from the deck of the keel. They gathered together under a warehouse, and sang and danced by the light of oil lanterns. I could not see very well, as it was dark on the wharves and their lanterns gave only a yellowish glow, but I could hear distinctly.

They danced to the music of a melodeon, a violin, and sometimes a mandolin. They sang very softly as they danced, and seemed to be enjoying themselves. Among the dark shapes I could see people of all ages, old and young, even babies, and I often wondered why they had come and where they were going, but I never had the chance to find out. A dock policeman was always at hand to make sure nobody mixed with them. I expect that was to prevent smuggling.

3 *Keelmen and their families*

My first recollection of life on a keel goes back to the time when I was five years old. My father fell into the canal, and since he could not swim, my mother had to fish him out with the boat-hook. Luckily the keel was not moving at the time, or he would have been drowned. I thought it was all very funny, but my father did not, for the canal was very cold.

As a boy I was very thin and small, with a fair complexion, blue eyes and almost white hair. Keelmen used to call me the 'White-Haired Kaffir', probably thinking of the White-Eyed Kaffir who was a singer on the music halls.

Most keelmen had nicknames. One keelman was always known as Nudger, because he had a bad habit of steering too close to other keels and just touching them. Another was called Makapenny because he was always looking for ways of making money. 'I could mak a penny outa that', he was always saying. Tug was so called because he would never sail the Humber, but was always towed by tug. I never knew any of their proper names, though I must have asked, for I was always a very inquisitive child. I liked to know how things like machinery, sails, trams or steamboats worked—and I still do.

All keelmen wore the same type of clothes, which were almost a uniform. Their navy blue jerseys were home knitted, with a diamond pattern on the front, and had high necks which fastened with two buttons on the left shoulder, so that the neck was never pulled out of shape. The fastening had to be on the left because we carried things on the right shoulder. These guernseys, as they

55

were called, had to be close-fitting and tight, since loose clothing could so easily have caught on projecting parts of keel or lock and pulled us overboard.

My mother always knitted ours in one piece on four needles, so that there were no seams, and even the sleeves, worked on three needles, were knitted into the garment. She used 14 or 15 oz of fine worsted wool from Hammond's in Hull for each guernsey, and she was such an expert knitter that it was difficult to tell the inside from the outside of the garment. To help to take the weight of the wool she always wore a knitting pad made of leather, stuffed with horsehair and with brass eyelet holes let into it. She tied this pad on to her waist with two tapes and slotted the needles not actually in use into the holes, so that the pad held the knitting for her. She never used a pattern. No one did. They all made it up as they went along—ropes and cables and knots and diamonds: all kinds of patterns. Some keelmen wore a silk hanky tied in a knot on top of their guernseys rather like a tie or cravat.

Our bell-bottomed trousers were made of brown corduroy ribbed with four narrow stripes then one wide one, and we always had them made to measure at Waistell's in Hull. We had a pair to work in and a pair for best. Sunday suits were very rare. In fact Dad had to cut his cords down for my brother and me, and Billy and I sewed them ourselves.

In very cold weather we wore short blue serge coats over the guernseys and cords. Again they had to be short and close-fitting, for a long coat would have been dangerous, always catching on things and throwing us overboard. We wore these coats for shopping trips, and when the weather was really bad we had oilskins, a coat, leggings and a sou'wester which tied under the chin. Father kept them in good condition by treating them with a mixture of linseed oil and soot to stop them cracking. He used the same mixture on the hatch covers.

Both men and boys wore soft cloth caps on their heads, since hats were useless, always blowing away in the wind. Some keelmen wore peaked caps like sea-going officers, but my Dad would have none of that. 'Big Heads!', he used to call them.

We never wore boots or clogs with nails or iron on them as they would have been too dangerous on the deck of the keel. We usually bought ordinary working boots made of leather and used them until they were worn out. Then we left them at a 'cloggers' at

Tinsley on our way up to Sheffield and collected them on our
way back. He gave them a wooden sole or 'clogged' them for us.

A small number of keelmen had their ears pierced because they
believed it would improve their sight. They wore plain gold ear-
rings called 'sleepers'. None of my relations had them, but there
is one old keelman in Thorne, Lewis Carter, who wears them to
this day.

Keelmen's wives had no special clothes. My mother always
wore a heavy woollen skirt, a cotton blouse, a knitted shawl and
high button boots when she was aboard. Her skirts and petticoats
were a great nuisance to her, always getting in the way and she
tucked them up behind her and fastened them with two safety
pins when she was hauling.

In rough weather she wore a little knitted scarf called a 'turn-
over' on her head. It was square but she folded it into a triangle,
pulled the two ends around the back of her head and tied them
over the point. It was as snug as a Balaclava.

The 'turn-over' was the only article of clothing that distin-
guished a keelwoman from anyone else. If a woman was wearing
one it was odds on that she was off a keel. Otherwise the women
were no different from those ashore.

Mother always had her best Sunday frock, hat and gloves with
her aboard the keel, and she wore this Sunday rig-out when
visiting friends or relations in the canal towns we passed through.
In fact she even wore them to go to her own house in Thorne.

Most keelwomen had fancy frocks for their weddings. Catherine
Ackroyd was married in a pale blue velvet frock with a pouched
front and tight leg o'mutton sleeves. The skirt had a big flounce
at the bottom and a frill around the hem. She wore a little black
hat with a black and white feather, and looked very smart.

In his unpublished manuscript, 'Stainforth Past and Present',
J. A. Himsworth describes a keelman's wedding in 1912: 'It was
a grand affair. The bride was taken to church in a cab pulled by
horses, but when the bride and groom came out of the church the
horses had been replaced by a line of keelmen who pulled the cab
around the village to the home of the bride. For this service they
were given gallons of beer paid for by the bridegroom.'

Although like most keelmen we had a house in Thorne, we lived
aboard on trips. Inside, the cabin was very cosy, the walls and
ceiling grained like oak or pine, with mahogany panels. Two sides

were lined with mahogany cupboards from locker tops to ceiling, and the lockers also served as seats. One locker was used for coal. It opened directly into the cabin from the hold so that we never had to carry coal about. We filled it up from the hold. On the third side was the fireplace, with a brass fender, and a small mantelpiece with a brass rail round it to keep the ornaments—two little dogs and a mirror—from dropping off. Behind the stove was a Yorkshire stone slab to stop the bulkhead catching fire, and beneath it was an iron plate for the same reason. Beside the fireplace were the steps leading up to the deck, and beneath them a door into the hold.

The fourth and starboard side of the cabin was taken up with a bunk-bed where mother and father slept. It was a bed in a cupboard, about 6 ft × 4 ft, so they had plenty of room. Babies were accommodated in baskets on the floor, and my brother and I bedded down in a cabin in the forecastle, which we shared with the gear and the anchor chains and with the fleets of trawlers I had painted on the walls. When it was rough in the Humber, however, we could not get into the forecastle at all, since water came over the bows, and we had to batten the hatch down.

The main cabin was at the aft end of the ship and was really quite small for living, eating and sleeping in, only about 6 ft × 5 ft, but it was compact and there was a place for everything. Inside the cupboards we kept our cleaning materials, pans and buckets, shoes and clothes. The centre cupboard at the aft end had glass doors, and Mother kept the tea and sugar in it. Because of being at the aft end of the boat, it was always called the transom cupboard, as everything at the aft end is called transom—transom beams, timbers, sails.

There were no windows, but two or three decklights, 8–9 in in diameter, let in plenty of light, and in summer one of them was unscrewed and fitted with a grid for extra ventilation. In winter a brass paraffin lamp swung from the ceiling.

We ate on a folding table, sitting on the locker tops. Except when we had visitors, we drank from mugs—there was no room for saucers—but we always had a cloth.

When mother was with us she did all the cooking on the little coal stove, so everything had to be fried or boiled. We ate a lot of bacon, ham and eggs for breakfast, stew, sea-pie, boiled meat and vegetables for dinner, and cold meat and pickles, plus any baking mother might have brought with her, such as jam and currant pasty or fruit pies, for tea. Supper was just a cup of tea and a piece of bread and jam or treacle.

Mother could bake only when she was at home, or when we were tied up at Kilnhurst Colliery, where there was a big lobby: a brick building with stone floors and two or three coal ovens. Later, some keels did have small ovens fitted into the forecastle. They held two small loaves, but made the cabin very hot.

We always had plenty of good fresh food, vegetables and fruit from the lock-keepers, who usually had a garden beside the canal, and milk and eggs from the farms all along our route. We always had a big ham to cut at from Hanneman's, the German pork butcher in Hull, and it rarely cost more than 4d or 5d a pound. This kept well and we usually saved it for when we ran out of fresh meat.

We sometimes stopped near Rotherham at a brewery called Mappins on the canal side at Masborough. There we picked up, not beer, but a gallon bottle of dandelion and burdock or sarsaparilla. It was a big earthenware bottle in a basketwork holder which fitted it very neatly, and we returned the empties on our journey back.

At Doncaster we always stopped at Parkinson's sweet factory, which was near the canal. We watched the men making rock but spent our money on broken butterscotch because it was better value.

When we delivered coal to the trawlers in Hull they generally gave us fish, and it was always the best. Any that was left over we put on the rigging, and when we went into other docks the gatemen would jump on board and get it, knowing it was for them.

Once an uncle who was a cook on a trawler gave us a great piece of beef which had been in a brine tub all the way to the White Sea and back. We soaked it in lots of water, then boiled it and it was delicious.

Fresh water was kept in a barrel called a water cask and fastened on deck. When we were in Hull docks and wanted it filled, we hoisted a bucket to the top of the mast, and the water-boat, a steam keel, would come and fill the cask for 6d. This steam keel supplied all the ships in the docks with drinking water, and carried between 40 and 50 tons, which it pumped out with a steam pump.

On the canals we got water at the collieries and the wharves, and in certain places we filled up with canal water, which was very

59

clean beyond Thorne and was called Bonny Ale—a name which was also given to the canal in those parts.

Our washing facilities were spartan. For Dad and me it was a bucket of canal water on deck, since fresh water was far too precious, and Mother washed in the cabin.

When we wanted a proper bath we used a long zinc or galvanized bath in the cabin. It was very comfortable in winter as we were always in front of a warm fire, which we had to have to heat the water but in the summer it was a sauna bath as well, since we had to close the cabin hatch in case anyone came on board. Lavatory arrangements were primitive, for there was no sanitation on Humber keels.

Every week Mother did her washing aboard with a small dolly tub and a wringer, and hung it on a line from the mast to the winch-posts above the hatches which covered the hold. If we were tied up in the canal we put two boat-hooks in the bank and slung a line between them. If it was raining and the hold was empty she could even hang it all in there to dry. She had to iron on the locker tops with flat irons.

Her really big wash, like her baking, she saved for Kilnhurst, which in addition to ovens had three coal coppers, tubs, mangles and scrubbing boards specially for the use of keelmen's wives. Whilst they washed and baked the keelmen unloaded the keels, and when that was done they swilled out the lobby floor and left everything ready for use again. Then there would be chinwagging until bedtime.

It was a hard life for a woman. Mother often had to steer the boat if Dad was busy with other jobs, and when there was no wind and no money to hire a horse, she had to help to haul the keel by hand: strenuous, grinding toil, which gave her a strangulated hernia.

She kept her cabin as clean as her little house in Thorne. She was always scrubbing the floor, washing the paintwork and cleaning the brasses, as well as knitting in her leisure time. And she was proud of the keel. She once met a fairground woman on the train from Mexborough to Kilnhurst. They had both been shopping and began to chat. The fairwoman said that she had always thought 'water gipsies' were dirty, and that made Mother very angry. Keelmen were never known as water gipsies and were ready to fight about it. Water gipsies to them were the people in the

narrow boats on the Leeds and Liverpool or Middlesex canals—
boats which only worked canals and never went into rivers or
around the coast like Humber keels. To be called a water gipsy,
as well as dirty, was too much for Mother, who challenged the
woman to inspect the keel. The fairwoman accepted the invitation
and was amazed at the spotless cabin. She took Mother back to
her caravan at the fairground, and Mother was equally amazed at
the clean and shining little home she had. Both had had a salutary
lesson, and Bill and I spent a joyful afternoon at the fair. There
were two sets of swings, two sets of dobby horses and a houpla
stall belonging to the fairwoman, and we had the run of them all—
for free!

We made the most of it, since we never had much time to play.
Only when we were moored to the quay for two or three weeks
was there any free time. Then we played football if there were
other boys around. Sometimes we boxed or fished, or played in
the hold. I even learned how to ride a bike in there, standing on
one pedal and pushing with the other foot to learn to balance, and
once ashore I was able to get on and ride away without any trouble.
Unfortunately I had never learned how to get off again, so I just
had to fall off, which didn't do the bike much good.

The hold was a good place on rainy days for other games:
marbles, shuttlecock and battledore, and even for hunt the thimble.

I had to work hard too, and from the age of five I learned to do
almost every job on a keel. Whenever the Humber was very rough,
Mother would take my brother to Thorne, and Dad and I would
manage the keel by ourselves. I enjoyed that. It was wonderful to
feel the wind and the sail, and to know that there was nothing but
Dad's knowledge and skill to get us where we wanted to go in that
vast river.

Then, a month before my twelfth birthday in June 1911 my
sister was born, and Mother decided never to go aboard the keel
again, so I became Dad's second man, and I worked with him until
I was fourteen, loving it in the summer and hating it in the winter.

Our day usually began at 4.30 in the morning when my first
job was to make the tea and fry the bacon for the horse marine.
Once I put the frying-pan full of bacon on the fire and fell asleep
again. Dad thought the keel was on fire when he saw smoke
pouring out of the hatch. I had to start again!

I thought it was a hard life. I was supposed to have the breakfast ready for when we got to a bridge or a lock, so that the horse marine could get on board for his meal. Then I had to go on to the towing bank and lead the horse until we came to the next lock or bridge. It was no good being half-asleep then, or I would have been pushed into the canal by the beast. I must have been dreaming one day when the horse rolled a bit sideways and pushed me off the bank. I was only wet up to the knees and it was a warm day, so it was not too bad. It could have been worse. That horse weighed about 10 cwt, and if she had rolled on me there wouldn't have been much of me left.

When I had had my turn at leading, I had to steer while Dad had his breakfast. I have steered the boat for hours, both in the Humber and in the canal.

When Dad had finished his breakfast it was at last my turn to eat, and afterwards I had to wash up for all of us, which I did after every meal. These eating arrangements were the same at midday, but at night we ate together after we had tied up. We usually arranged to be at a town or village by nightfall, or at a lock in a canal. If we could not reach any of these places we would put a 'dog's leg'—it looked like half an anchor—into the bank, and if we were in the river and not in the canal we dropped anchor.

After washing up, I had to wash down the keel and clean up the cabin, the work my mother had done when she was aboard, but I was soon back to men's work. I've pushed the keel along with a boat-hook; I've pulled it in a seal, and I've helped to heave her out of the mud when she got stuck.

In my spare time I had to mend sails. A new sail lasted fifteen or twenty years if looked after, and we looked after ours. I also made fenders, which we hung over the side at the bows and stern to stop the keel being damaged in the locks. We made them by sewing three or four lengths of old towrope together with a marline spike and a thin cotton rope, usually an old man-line. Turk's Heads were round, and made by passing the thin rope in and out, almost like darning a sock. I could make two kinds. Some keelmen could make fancy fenders by splicing and plaiting. They looked very nice but were more for ornament than use. We sometimes bought fenders which were round and full of cork and we used them in the same way, to protect our keels when entering locks and bridges or passing other keels. Always in the Humber we lifted them on deck to reduce resistance as they dragged in the water.

An extra job I did was to collect fresh watercress from the freshwater drains at Keadby, and fill Mother's washtub. Then we gave it to the dock gatemen at the fish dock. Little gifts like this helped us to keep the goodwill of the men, who, if they didn't like you, could keep you hanging about outside the dock gates, bumping up and down for an hour and a half or more. It was always calm inside the dock, and some dock-masters were nasty and kept keels outside at the jetty on purpose.

Another of my jobs was to go errands. We would tie up at a canal town or moor in the docks, and I would run into the nearest shops and put the shopping in a bundle handkerchief, a square of blue and white linen which tied up by the four corners so that I could slip it over my arms and leave my hands free for climbing up and down ladders or the large nails driven into the wooden piles supporting the jetties. Sometimes I had to carry it in my mouth so that I could climb up and down ropes when the keel was too far away from the steps. The water in the river Hull used to go down, and the keel would slide as far away from the banks as the ropes would permit and lie on the mud.

I wasn't always a good provider. Once, when Dad sent me ashore in Hull, for the dinner, he said, 'If you bring sausages and tomatoes I'll throw you in the river!' I must have been feeding him on nothing else for weeks, as they were easy for me to cook. Dad liked to make a sea-pie himself. We had a big oval iron pan into which he would put a rabbit, stewing beef and all the vegetables we had. It was cooked slowly on the fire, and then Dad made a suet dumpling the size of the pan, and we really gorged ourselves.

Once I went shopping in Hull leaving the keel at St. Andrew's Dock, but I didn't get back in time to catch it, as a tug had towed it away. I had to walk five miles to catch up again, carrying the food, as I had no money for tram fares. Dad thought it was funny, but I didn't! When you are only twelve years old, five miles is a long way.

At Medgehall I had to leave the keel, cross by a little footbridge over a drain, and go to the farm for our eggs. I always had to wait while the farmer's wife collected them fresh from the nest, but it was worth it as they were only 1s for two dozen and she always gave me an extra one for myself. Of course Dad couldn't stop sailing in order to wait for me, so then I had to get into the coggy boat and scull like mad to catch up with him. That keel could move with a good wind behind it, and I was tired out with sculling, and so was Dad with laughing when I finally reached it and got back on board.

When the *Mary Ward* was auctioned off because her owner had died, Dad would have liked to buy her, but he had no money, so she had to go and then he was out of work for a time and so was I.

He went 'purchasing', as it was called. That was going between Hull and Keadby as an extra man. The Humber Keel Trust stipulated that every keel had to have two men aboard in the Humber. It was this wage that I had saved my parents, as the Trust did not say what age the man had to be! I had been their 'second man' from the age of six until I was twelve. Purchasing was poorly paid, so Dad got a job laying gas mains at Thorne for a time, until a man offered him another keel and then we were off again.

Our new keel was called the *Intrepid* and belonged to a carrying agent in Hull. It was known as the 'bagboat' and was much smaller than the one we were used to. It had a regular trade taking wheat to Sheffield and collecting all the empty bags from the mills on the way back to Hull. All grain was in bags then, 18 st to the bag. We would take the bags from over the side of the ships in Hull docks, and Dad would have to carry and stow each bag as it came down. He was only 5 ft 4 in and 10 st in weight so it was very hard work for him. If we started to load at six o'clock in the morning, we would get through 1,000 by teatime. The docks worked from 6 a.m. to 6 p.m. in those days, with an hour from 8 to 9 a.m. for breakfast, and another break from 12 to 1 for dinner. My job while Dad was loading was to attend to the ropes, as the ship would be steadily lifting out of the water while the keel sank deeper with the weight of the grain.

After stowing it all we had to cover up, batten down and get to the lockhead ready for going up river the next morning. The *Intrepid* had no sails, so it was tugs in the Humber and horses in the canal.

The tugs belonged to William Gray & Co, and all of them had -*man* at the end of their names: *Welshman*, *Boatman*, *Riverman*, *Krooman* and *Fenman*. The one I remember best was the *Fenman*. She was of light draught for towing in the Trent and occasionally

11. A keelman's wedding

12. The *Day Star*

13. A horse marine taking his horse to the stables

14. The Old House lock, Tinsley

even in the Keadby Canal as far as Thorne. She had her tow-hooks placed amidships to help her round the sharp bends, whereas most tugs had their hooks about a third of the length of the tug frame.

Gray's company later became part of the United Towing Company along with the other tug-owners. They had docking tugs, one at each end of a ship to take her into dock and berth her. They had sea-going tugs too: the *Englishman*, *Frenchman* and *Seaman*.

The United Towing Company is still in existence. Before it was formed there were several tug-owners in Hull. The Wilson Line had their own tugs as well as a large fleet of seagoing ships of between 8,000 and 10,000 tons. All their ships had names ending in *-o*. The *Odesso*, *Marengo*, *Othello* and *Bayardo*. The *Bayardo* was a cargo passenger ship which ran a regular service between Hull and the Continent, taking passengers and bringing in fruit and dairy produce. She was a fast ship, known on the river as the 'greyhound of the Humber'. But once she tried to reach Hull in a fog, and struck the middle sandbank where she broke her back and became a total loss. Although no lives were lost it was the end of a fine ship. She gradually sank into the sand and was then blown up by explosives until she finally disappeared.

The sailing keel was beginning to die out too. Some keels were given engines which ran on paraffin although they were started by petrol or a cartridge or even a blowlamp. Some keels ran on petrol alone and there were a few steam-keels although I can remember only the *Swift*, the *Swiftsure* and the *Carabinese*. She was owned by Hewett's Brewery of Grimsby, and usually called the 'beer-boat' because she loaded barrels and cases of bottled beer and discharged them at a wharf next to Hanley's flour mill at Doncaster.

She had vertical boilers, a small engine to drive the propeller and a small wheelhouse as she was steered by wheel. This method of steering was not suitable for sailing keels and we envied the crew their cosy wheelhouse, so much more comfortable to be in than the exposed deck of a sailing keel. There was only the head of the man above the wheelhouse top and he never got his legs and feet wet as we did. Our foredeck was often under water for long periods and even on a fine day, if it was rough, we could be wet up to our knees.

The mast and funnels on the steam-keels were hinged so that they could be lowered to go under the railway bridges at Thorne.

ALH—E

65

They were independent of tides, winds, tugs and horses and sometimes in a head wind rack they would give our keel a tow.

It was hard work on the bagboat and not very rewarding, so when, early in 1914 I told my father that I had decided not to be a keelman he was not surprised and said he thought I could do better at something else. He had never realized his lifelong ambition to own a keel and it had been a great disappointment to him.

4 Ashore

I went to Thorne to look for a job. I knew the town quite well because I had often stayed there with my grandparents when I was a little boy and at our own house when we were 'fettling'. We always stopped for a week or two in summer to paint and clean everything on the keel and this was called 'fettling'. We tied up in West Street, as near to our house as possible, and painted and repaired everything we could. We took everything to pieces. Even the windlass and the rollers and all the fenders were removed, chipped, scraped and greased before being put back. We could do these jobs in the hold in bad weather, and when it was fine we painted the entire keel.

Thorne was a quiet country town before the colliery came to Moorend, or Moorends as we called it, and many people were against the sinking of the pit shaft because they thought it would spoil the place, as indeed it did in my opinion, but there's no stopping progress. Thorne had fine land for growing potatoes, and it was noted for its celery, which flourished in the peaty soil. Many peas were also grown in the area.

We had lived in Plantation Road for a while, and then in Carter Lane, where we had a two-bedroomed house with a living room with oven and sink but no tap water. We brought water in from a pump in the lane and filtered it for drinking. There was a front room which overlooked the garden, and at the back was an orchard, full of fruit trees as well as red and black currants.

But the house I remember best was in Ellison Street. It was one of the first in the town to have tap water, and even then the tap was at the bottom of the garden. We had our own dry lavatory and gas lighting when many other houses shared lavatories and used paraffin lamps.

My mother's mother, Grandma Williamson, lived quite near to us. She had a small general shop at the opposite corner of West Street, and it had a huge garden and two stables where she let me keep pigeons, which Uncle George, my mother's brother, used to feed for me when we were away. I ended up with over 200, so was forced to let them go.

George was the only member of the family who had been well educated. He had been to the Bluecoat School in Lincoln and was a good scholar. Even so, he was only a part-time postman, who looked after Grandma's garden and sold morning papers from a rickety old handcart. He never finished delivering the morning round until two o'clock in the afternoon but no one seemed to mind. He and his cart were known all over Thorne as he was always cheerful and full of character. He once traced our family tree and found we had ancestors who sailed in the whaling fleet from Hull.

Grandad Williamson was a keelman, and although he came from Lincoln, he lived in Thorne all the time that I knew him.

His brother Charlie had also been a keelman for a time but left home to go on tugs, towing Tom Puddings. Then he left the life altogether and became the landlord of The Royal Sovereign on the Queen's Dockside in Hull. Another brother, Uncle Jack, was a keelman too—so that was most of the family.

My father's father, Lemon Bill, was a keelman as well. He was a keen Wesleyan, and was always known as Lemon Bill. He lived in a big house called Walnut Tree House in Queen Street, and was the captain of two wooden keels: the *Comet* and the *Triumph*.

When at home I always attended church on Sunday morning, and as I often delivered the morning papers to the vicarage for my Uncle George, I got to know the vicar quite well. His housekeeper always gave me a toffee for the paper, and he was always kind to me. He was a bachelor called Canon Littlewood, a grand man, loved by everybody, though even he could be out of touch. He once met my mother in the street and told her what a nice, polite little boy I was—which just shows that he didn't really know me!

The odd thing was that whenever I stayed with my mother's mother I always went to the Salvation Army with her, attended their Sunday School, and even walked with them playing the tambourine. Then when I stayed with my father's father, I attended the Wesleyan Chapel, as did most keelmen. My grandfather was so keen that he once held a service aboard his keel while it was moored at Thorne, and old keelmen still remember the occasion.

What a mixture I was! Part Wesleyan, part Salvation Army and part Anglican. I suppose it was inevitable that I should marry a Roman Catholic!

I may have gone to church regularly but I seldom went to school. My first recollection of school was when I was about eight years old when we were frozen up for seven weeks, and my mother took my brother and me to the Thorne Travis Charity School, which I liked very much, though my brother screamed all day.

The longest spell of education I ever had was a period of three months when I was nine years old. The teacher, Miss Woodcock, sent us outside to look at the wrought-iron church gates, and then to draw them. My drawing was pinned up on the school wall because it was the best in the class, but then, I've always liked drawing ships or birds or animals, but never people.

I once had another spell of three weeks in school at Keadby while we were waiting for a cargo of coal. This time the teacher asked us to draw a pot duck which she kept on her desk. My picture was taken round to all the teachers in the school, and the headmaster gave me a penny. For once I was on top of the world! But that wasn't the end of the episode. He then came to see my parents on the keel, and offered to keep me with him at his house so that I could have an education. He would have made no charge for my food; in fact the only thing he asked of my parents was that they should clothe me. He thought I should make a good draughtsman, and might perhaps eventually find a job in the drawing office of the Great Central Railway. I was very excited, but my parents could not afford to let me go as I was too handy on the keel and saved them the expense of hiring a man. I was disappointed, but that was when I first learnt that it was no good wanting something you could not have.

I never went to school in Rotherham or Sheffield, as the other keelmen's children told us that the teachers there couldn't be bothered with us since they could not hope to teach us much in two or three weeks. That I could understand. In any case the schools near the canals or rivers where we moored were very rough, and the local children often ganged up on us and called us 'keely dogs'.

I once went for some fish and chips in Sheffield, and a gang of lads collected outside, waiting for me to come out. I was on my own and small for my eleven years. The man in the shop wrapped the supper up well and told me to button it up inside my waistcoat and run. I ran all right, while he held them off. Luckily I could run fast so they did not catch me, but the fish and chips were in a mixed-up state when I finally got on board the keel. I didn't find the incident funny at the time, but I've laughed since.

We were better off in Hull where we had more contact with people like dockers, stevedores and dock gatemen, and where we were usually known as 'keelies'.

Anyhow, for one reason or another I got no more than six months' education in my whole life, which is one reason why I tried to give my daughters as much schooling as possible. It is a great handicap in life to be a poor scholar, as I found out later on. I always enjoyed the time I spent at school.

I learnt to read and write in hospital when I was ten years old. I had a very bad attack of sickness while we were at Kilnhurst Colliery, and as there was no doctor there Dad had to go to Mexborough for one, and when he finally arrived he diagnosed appendicitis. I had to go to the nearest hospital, which was at Doncaster, and as I was not allowed to go by road Dad had to sail the keel there, and then take it all the way back to Kilnhurst by himself for a load of coal.

We arrived at eight o'clock at night, and I was laid on a board in the cab that took me to hospital so that I should not be bent in any way. The operation was supposed to be performed immediately but they kept me for nine weeks, feeding me on milk and Benger's Food. I have disliked milk ever since and cannot take it, even in tea.

I could never sleep at night there, partly because the boy in the next bed slept with his eyes open, which fascinated me and scared me at the same time, so the night nurses passed the time in teaching me to read and write. I have much to thank that hospital for.

When they finally operated (and I can remember walking downstairs to the theatre, and even climbing up on to the operating table) they found an abscess as big as a hen's egg. I was lucky to be alive.

I enjoyed those hospital days. I was there for fourteen weeks from October to December, and had turkey for Christmas dinner for the first time in my life. It was my first day on a full diet, and I ate so much I nearly burst.

When I was convalescing I spent a lot of time in the men's ward, where there were nine miners—a grand set of men who were very kind to me. It became my job to take them the opening mixture, and the sight of their faces as it approached made me grin all over my face. There was 'White Mary', which was nasty but not very strong, and 'Black Jack', which was both, and also castor oil, the worst of all.

As I grew stronger I had the run of the hospital, which was a converted private house. Sometimes I went into the kitchen to help the maids to dry the pots, and earned an orange for my labour. Sometimes I whistled down the tube to the kitchen and hauled up the beef tea on a handlift. Sometimes I just rolled bandages on a little machine fitted to the side of my cot.

During my stay in hospital my mother lived with Aunt Trotty at Balby, so Dad had to do the best he could with the keel on his own. It must have been a trying time for my parents with both the extra work and the extra expense. When at last I was discharged Mother, Billy and I went to our house in Thorne for another two months, as I was still an out-patient. The family doctor warned my parents that I should never be strong enough for hard work, and ought to be educated for office work, but he didn't know the stuff keelmen were made of. Since then I have had some of the hardest jobs there are, and have played rugby football without ill effects.

My formal education may have been scanty but there was always plenty to do, see and learn in Thorne although it was such a quiet little town. What industry there was was connected with keels in one way or another. One of my favourite spots was the keel-building yard. There were two yards on the banks of the canal. One was called Dunston's, a yard which celebrated its hundredth anniversary in June 1958. The other one was called Staniland's where two of my father's younger brothers worked. Neither of them had wanted to work on keels but they had not managed to get away from them either. I sometimes watched them cutting up trees by hand. It was a long process. They placed the tree over the pit, with one man underneath it and the other on top, then they sawed away with a big, two-handled saw, pulling the blade up and down between them. It was hard work, and it took two days to cut up one large tree. The woods most commonly used were the hard woods like oak, ash and elm but occasionally woods already cut into planks or deals like larch, mahogany, pine and redwood were imported.

The yards were busy places but very quiet in comparison with present-day shipyards. There was the noise of the sawing and the hammering it is true, but the banging was with wooden mallets and long nails called spikes. The whole yard smelled of freshly sawn wood, boiling pitch, new paint, tar and new ropes.

Carpenters actually built the keel, and the mast and block-makers made the mast. They were usually of fir but if you couldn't get one big enough a baulk, or 12 in square of pine, was used. The bottom was left square to fit the lutchet and the mast-maker trimmed the corners with an axe and an adze and then shaped and tapered the baulk with a drawknife and a spokeshave. He used callipers to measure the diameter.

When the keel was complete it had to be caulked and pitched to make it watertight. First of all oakum, which is tarry rope teased out to the fineness of fluff, was rolled slackly into lengths and driven into V-shaped cuttings between the planks by a carpenter using steel tools and a special wooden mallet. A very narrow tool was used at first to drive the oakum as far as it could go; then a wider tool was used for the second layer of oakum and a third and even wider tool finished it off.

Boiling pitch was poured into the grooves with a pointed ladle and allowed to set. Finally the surplus pitch was scraped off.

On the side planking the pitch was rubbed on with a pitch mop and some decks were done with Stockholm tar instead of pitch as, although expensive, it never set really hard and so was less liable to crack and never ran in the sun.

The painters then took over the keel and finally the testers who checked the compartments for leaks.

When a keel was ready for launching the carpenters put it on the slipways. Then they put poles on the deck, flying the Merchant Navy flag (Red Ensign) at one end, the Union Jack at the other, and the burgee (the flag with the ship's name on it) in the middle. Sometimes they even decorated the keel with a string of flags from end to end.

The keel was usually christened by a member of the owner's family who broke a bottle of wine over its bows. A small crowd often gathered to watch the launch but they were careful to stand well away from the opposite hauling banks, for the keels were launched sideways and when they hit the water a huge wave splashed over the canal banks.

Since a canal, unlike a river, is not affected by tides the launching ceremony could be held at any time the owners desired. Sometimes they had to travel from Hull, or even further away, but the launches generally took place at 3 p.m. as very little work was done in the yard afterwards.

A man was stationed at each end of the keelbuilding yard to warn oncoming vessels, and the masts, sails and rigging were put on after the launch so that they were not damaged.

When all was finished the owners and the builder went into the offices for a drink and the workmen went into the carpenters' shop where a barrel of beer was provided for their celebration.

The size of the keel was determined by the locks and bridges on the canal where it was intended to trade, and the size of the mast and sails by the size of the keel. The larger the keel the more sail it could carry.

The shipyards would build a keel to any specification, though of course a firm on a small canal could not build a really large keel. Both Thorne yards could make keels of any size, from Sheffield keels like ours (90–100 tons) to smaller vessels of 80–100 tons. Dunston's even made Humber sloops, which were bigger than Humber keels.

Each yard had its own little trademarks or way of doing things, and a keelman in those days could walk on any keel and tell you where it had been built.

Occasionally if a keel needed repairing, the carpenters, instead of putting in a new plank, would do some 'doubling'. This meant sticking a new plank over the top of the old one, and they used 'buggarum' to stick the two together. First, the new plank was steamed in a steamer box to the shape required, and carried to the keel well wrapped in bags so that the men were not scalded. It had to be fastened to the stem with clamps, then bent round and stuck

73

with the 'buggarum'. This was a real brew, consisting of linseed-oil settlings, flocks, sometimes a little straw or hay, and dollops of horse manure. It was spread with a flat piece of wood, and oddly enough it wasn't unpleasant to handle, and smelled chiefly of the linseed oil.

Fred Bisby, a well-known keelman in Thorne, says that when a clinker built keel needed its bottom caulking, they stripped everything off the keel, filled it with empty barrels and turned it upside down so that they could caulk it downhand instead of overhead.

At Dunston's there was a ropery, and I often watched the man and the boy there making ropes for towing keels. They worked outside all day, whether it was wet or fine.

The ropemaker took a bundle of bassy, hemp or manilla, looped it round his waist and twisted it into a thin yarn about $\frac{1}{4}$ in in diameter. The end of this he attached to a wheel turned by the boy. While the ropemaker walked backwards along the ropewalk, twisting the yarns into a strand as he went, the boy turned the wheel, so putting in the twist.

The ropewalk was about $\frac{1}{4}$ mile in length, and every so often there were posts with hooks where he could lay the strands to keep them off the ground. When a number of strands had been made in this way he would fasten them together on another wheel and repeat the procedure, twisting the narrow strands into one larger one of about 1 in in diameter. Six of these, twisted together, made the tough and springy towrope of a keel about 4 or 5 in thick and the largest rope we used.

The ropery had been very important at one time and had supplied all the surrounding countryside with ropes of coir, hemp, manilla and cotton.

There was a sail-loft at Dunston's too: a light, airy room above the stairs, smelling of tarry twine and the beeswax used to soften the twine for sewing. The room had an outside stairway and long windows down one side. The sailmaker was a skilled man. He cut out the white unbleached cotton for the sails, and sat cross-legged on the floor to stitch them. They were too big to be made in one piece, and so strips were sewn together. He wore a piece of leather over his palm, with an iron disk just below his first finger to help push the needle through the cloth. Every stitch he made was even, and he moved very swiftly along the sail and along the sail-loft floor.

The yard seemed to make everything a sailing ship needed from

74

the top to the bottom, or as we used to say, 'from the truck (the little cap on the mast head) to the keel'.

Another industry connected with keels was tar and pitch distilling at the pitchworks by the side of the canal. The men there took coal-tar from the gasworks, boiled it, added chemicals and let it run into pitchponds while it was hot. The ponds were square or oblong, about 4 ft deep and lined with bricks. When the pitch had set solid it was dug out and used for caulking the seams in keels and wooden ships to make them watertight. It was also used for roads and flat roofs.

My father and I once took 100 tons of this pitch to Hull for export to America. We had it on the keel for about a week, and our skins turned yellow, but otherwise it did not seem to do us much harm. It smelled very strongly of coal-tar, and made our eyes water in strong light.

There was a brewery in Thorne, but no other industry except farming and shipping at Waterside, the old port on the river Don. Keels and sloops used to come up the river there from Hull and York, but I can't remember much about the port. If we got as far as that in my young days we'd emigrated!

I had few hobbies as I never had time for them, but I did like birds. I once kept a thrush's nest full of eggs, which had been abandoned by the mother, in our back kitchen, hoping they would hatch. They didn't, and when mother knocked them down you couldn't bear it in the house for the smell. I was more successful with young thrushes, and raised many a one, feeding them on worms until they could fly away.

I had some time for games. We played football, marbles, relieve-O (a chasing game well known to children in the north), follow the leader, whip and top, hide and seek, and catch and run. Mostly I played with the four children of the man who lived next door and owned my father's keel. The son was my own age and we were great friends. When he came home from school at teatime he had to go out with a box on wheels to collect horse-droppings, and all us lads used to help him so that he could have his tea and come out to play a bit earlier. His father sold the manure to a gardener for 6d a box, and if the lad was lucky he got a new pair of boots with the profit. He kept himself and his three sisters in boots that way. The girls wore high-buttoned boots, which I thought looked very nice.

Ashore

The children had no mother, and since their father was crippled, they were very poor. Their diet consisted mainly of bread, butter and jam made from the fruit in their own orchard. When their father died too and the keel was sold, the money was given to a family friend who had a small dairy farm. He and his wife became the children's foster parents, although they had four boys and a girl of their own. The money helped to keep them for a time, and the eldest girl soon went into domestic service.

Treats for any of us were few: a visit to relatives in one of the canal towns where we were moored, and perhaps a day trip on the ferryboat from Hull Pier to Cleethorpes in the summer was all we expected.

We particularly liked going to see my mother's sister Jane, who lived in Conisborough, and we often went to stay there for Christmas. Uncle Livesey was a miner at Cadeby Main Colliery. His job was to cut out the stone whenever the miners came to a fault between the seams. It was such a dangerous job that Aunt Jane always kept his bedroom spotless and ready—in case he had an accident. Dangerous or not, he earned so little that he had to make extra money by carting, ploughing, and even collecting night soil with his cart and two or three horses.

They lived in a country cottage in the middle of a chalk quarry. All around the sides of the quarry, Uncle had flowers growing, and chickens had free range all around the house. It was a grand spot and we loved it there. We usually had a fine Christmas dinner, with a chicken and perhaps a rabbit as well, followed by home-boiled ham, with plenty of home-baked pastries and custards for tea.

For presents I sometimes got a clockwork toy, with an apple, an orange and some nuts, or perhaps some new clothes, a cap, a pair of socks or a new guernsey.

We never thought about birthdays. I don't even remember having one! I suppose we were given a pair of boots or trousers, or something that we needed.

Another auntie lived at Mexborough, and we often had a day there when we passed through. I liked going, because her husband worked at the glassworks making ginger-pop bottles: the type with glass marbles and rubber rings. We replenished our stock of marbles on those visits! We couldn't stay overnight, as their home was a 'one up and one down' with a ladder to the bedroom. The yard was covered with cinders, and was a real mess in bad weather.

They were so poor that Aunt Bee ran a home coal business of her own. I remember her as a gaunt, hard-working woman, who lived a tiring life with three children to bring up.

A summer day trip to Cleethorpes was an adventure. Sometimes we went by train from Thorne South Station by the Great Central Railway, or the 'Mucky, Slushy and Lousy' as we cheekily called it. You could jump out of the window, set a packet of seeds and pick the flowers on the way back, the journey was so slow. If we were moored in Hull we crossed the Humber by ferryboat and then caught an even slower train.

Cleethorpes was not developed as a resort in those days. It was just a seaside town with a few roundabouts and donkeys on the sands, and a two-wheel pony cart that obligingly took you for a ride down to see the sea, quite a distance when the tide was out. In fact I have been there for a day without seeing it at all. But we enjoyed the pier, the shellfish stalls, and of course the fish and chips. The trip was the highlight of our summers.

Going to Hull was always exciting. Sometimes my mother took my brother and me to East Park, where we could go on the swings, play ball, watch the boats on the lake, feed the ducks and then walk the mile back to the keel.

If we visited friends in Hull we had to walk home through the dark side streets along the dockside, quite close to where an old man o' war was moored in the Humber. It was a prison ship called the *Southampton*, full of young convicts training to be seamen. We thought it mysterious and frightening.

'I don't envy you your walk home', Mother's friend always said as we were leaving after supper. We never looked forward to it ourselves, and our dangers were not over when we finally reached the keel for we had to climb down the straight steel rungs, let into the sides of the docks without handholds, and then jump aboard from the bottom rungs, which were always wet and slippery. Sometimes we had a plank from the keel resting on them, but if we didn't have one long enough we just had to jump, or walk a sort of tightrope on two boat-hooks, difficult to manoeuvre in daylight, never mind at night.

When at last we were aboard we were always a little apprehensive in case the keel had been broken into during our absence, for the docks were full of queer characters, and we had thief bars fitted across our hatchway, as well as the lock.

77

One keelman bought himself a pistol to scare away these intruders, who sometimes dossed down on the decks of the keels. One night he challenged strange footsteps and then took a shot, missing his own son by inches. The bullet went through the bulkhead, and the young man dropped down from shock.

From the age of twelve I began to get pocket money. I helped to stow coal, wash the keel or run errands for other keelmen, and they generally gave me 6d. I spent all my money on books. I was very keen on adventure stories, and enjoyed *The Last of the Mohicans*, *The Count of Monte Cristo*, *Twenty Thousand Leagues Under the Sea*, and a weekly magazine called *Cheer, Boys, Cheer*. But I read everything I could lay my hands on, from dictionaries to encyclopedias, and I once tackled a weighty tome called *British Colonization and Empire*.

I enjoyed the theatre, too: in Sheffield the Empire and Lyceum, in Rotherham the Empire, in Mexborough the Royal, in Doncaster the Empire, and in Hull the Tivoli and Alexandra, the Hippodrome and Empire, as well as the Circus. The Circus had the first moving pictures, or 'living pictures' that I ever saw. We watched in complete darkness whilst the pictures danced and flickered on the screen. At the end of every roll of film there would be a long wait whilst the next one was being fitted. The pianist went mad, playing all the time and trying to fit the music to the picture.

In October Hull held a great fair which ran for a whole week and stretched from Anlaby Road to Cottingham Road, filling Walton Street and the fairground, about eleven acres in all. It was said to be the biggest fair in the north of England, though not as famous as the Blaydon Race Fair or the Nottingham Goose Fair.

The streets were full of fortune-tellers and palmists, who hired the front rooms of the houses on Walton Street, where the small gardens too were often rented out to side-shows. We enjoyed the dobby horses, the helter skelters and the cake walks, but my favourite was Over the Falls. You went in and were immediately swept off your feet for about twenty yards on a canvas sheet which rocked and shook and threw you all over the place. Everything took place in semi-darkness too—to spare the girls' blushes.

Outside you had to walk the gauntlet of coconut shies, aunt Sallies, shooting booths, boxing booths, menageries and circus tents—all demanding your money—while the sweet-sellers, with brandy-snap, nougat, toffee apples, chips and hot peas also tempted it from your pockets. It was a noisy, raucous scene but all alive. No bingo and no slot machines!

By far the biggest event in our lives was Thorne Fair week, and we looked forward to it for months. Mother's sisters and her brother always came to stay with us, and though it was a bit of a squash, we all enjoyed ourselves.

The week before the fair, Mother always stayed at home to wash everything that could possibly be washed, and to have the baking day of all baking days. She made bread, pastries, meat pies and currant pies as well as boiling our usual ham and roasting a beef joint of 7 or 8 lb.

The Fair started on Monday, 11 June, or the nearest Monday to it, with a gipsy horse fair in South Parade, where horses were bought and sold, gipsies haggled and sometimes fought, and we lads sat on the walls and watched the fun—well out of reach.

Jugglers were there too, entertaining the crowds with their tricks. One, dressed as a Red Indian, was especially clever. He threw up an opened umbrella instead of the usual ball or clubs, and while it was coming down juggled with a pipe and a cigar.

Of course there was always a strong man, dressed in a leopard skin with one strap over the shoulder. He bent iron bars over his knees and twisted nails with his hands, and sometimes challenged the crowd to beat him, but I never saw anyone succeed.

The cheap-jacks really had the gift of the gab. They could persuade the crowd to buy anything. Useless articles and medicines for every conceivable complaint were sold with ease. One chap had pills that cured 'boils, spots, pimples and scabby eyebrows'. Another made cough lozenges 'right in front of your eyes' on a little paraffin stove. He boiled up the herbs and poured his mixture into little tin trays to set. He always sold a lot, even though it was the middle of summer, but then they were very tasty and cheap at 2d a bag, and we all liked them.

A third sold knife sharpeners and celluloid eyeglasses that could be used either as binoculars or magnifying glasses. Others sold penknives, and an Indian, complete with turban and silk jacket, sold scarves and pieces of real silk.

Patter was always entertaining. 'We're not here and gone to-morrow,' they assured us. 'No, you're going tonight!' we shouted back.

Not on the programme of events were the fist fights which always broke out somewhere or other, and we watched with glee.

Side-shows and amusements were held in the Market Place and the Green. We had two sets of roundabouts in the Market Place, dobby horses, and Corrigan's farm animals, which went round and round and up and down just like the horses, but consisted of pigs, cows, cockerels, dogs and donkeys. Each roundabout had its own musical organ and traction engine to tow it from town to town. I always enjoyed the engines more than the roundabouts. In the Green were the boxing booths, with boxers encouraging challenges from the locals. Our home-grown toughies usually got a good hiding! There were also goals where you could have a go with footballs, a very popular pastime.

The cattle shows and handicraft exhibitions were held on the Wednesday. Cattle were judged out in the open air, in pens, and the handicrafts were held in marquees. As country people, we had a lot to contribute. There was knitting, crocheting and embroidery and home-made clothes, as well as contests for the best home-baked bread, pastry, jams, pickles, wines, beers, butter and curds. People were very keen to win the prizes for the best three in each class.

Thursday was gala day, with a brass band playing marches and *Poet and Peasant* or the *1812 Overture*, and a troupe of performing cavalry. All this took place in Foster's Field, now the park. There were pony races too, but only amateur riders were allowed to compete, and as we knew most of them, this added to the fun. We could have a laugh when they took a tumble, and give a cheer when a favourite won.

There was show jumping, and trotting races with horses pulling very light carriages. Local lads, including me, made 3d, or even 6d extra money by meeting the trotting horses at the station and pulling the carriages to the stables at the back of Foster's Hall.

I earned money, too, by going to the station and carrying visitors' luggage, or rather pulling it on a two-wheeled box. There were plenty of customers, for the North Eastern Railway used to run a special cheap day trip to Thorne on the Saturday of Fair Week. With these tips and the 6d Mother gave me I was quite well off, and I never spent all my money on the Fair, although I did enjoy the ice cream, the sweets, the roundabouts and the aunt Sallies.

By way of entertainment there was once a balloon ascent, and

15. Stainforth Aquatic Sports Committee

16. Sculling race for keelmen's wives

17. The greasy pole

18. Keels moored at Stainforth during Fair Week

a woman came down in a parachute. Unfortunately she floated a good way off, and the show people had to gallop after her in a pony and trap. The balloon came down nearby, as the woman had opened the gas valve before jumping.

That night there was a grand firework display with set pieces of farm animals and the head of the king. It was exciting, but I enjoyed most watching the men put them together in the loft at the Hall.

The best day was Friday, because it was our day: the day of the keelmen's water sports. The whole of the week was a holiday for keelmen, and every keel in the district was decorated with strings of flags and moored at Thorne. The sports were run by the keelmen themselves, with their headquarters at The Canal Tavern. The Canal Company allowed them to charge for admission to the hauling banks near the canal bridge where spectators gathered to watch the fun.

The sports began at 1.30 and lasted until 7.30 or even 8, and the first event was always a sculling race for men in the keels' coggy boats, using one oar. The second was a similar race for keelmen's wives and daughters. With a lot of splashing and laughing they made good times, considering the fact that they were wearing their best dresses and high button boots.

One of the best races was the tub race. For this we used barrels cut in half. The keelmen sat in the tubs and paddled them like canoes, but unlike canoes the tubs often turned over, or just filled with water and sank.

For the dobby-horse race we sat astride the barrels and paddled with a double-ended paddle. The barrels had weights in the bottom and wooden horse-heads at the front. It was difficult even to stay on these 'cock-horses', and in fact if you did manage to stay upright, you most probably won the race.

Paddling races came next, with six men to a coggy boat, all paddling with their hands. They had to draw lots for the boats, as keel coggy boats were used for the occasion, and these were of different sizes and weights. It was a race in which there was a lot of splashing and it ended in a ducking, as indeed did all the others.

In the swimming races there were always so many entrants that both the 50 and 100 yds had three or four heats before the final, and in my day a one-legged man called Ralph Speight was unbeatable.

ALH—F

81

The highlight of the afternoon was the Greasy Pole, for which a 25 ft pole, well greased with soft soap and tallow, was set horizontally over the canal from a raised platform on a crane on the hauling bank. It had a flag at the end, and the first man to walk the length of the pole and seize the flag was the winner. It was a dangerous sport. If two or more managed to get the flag before falling into the water, there was a 'walk-off' and for this they had to walk upright.

The water sports ended with a fancy-dress parade for the keelmen's children who, dressed as jockeys or policemen, clowns or old-time characters, made a dry ending to the day.

Ours were not the only water sports, for keelmen held them at Stainforth too, as well as at Hull where, because they were held on the river, the date varied to fit in with the tides.

On the Saturday, the last day of the Fair, there were the keelmen's land sports, held in the fairground by arrangement with the Fair people. There were sprints, mile and half-mile races, and unusual events like tilting the bucket, in which a bucket was nailed to a board with a hole in it. When the bucket was full of water, the board was balanced on two upright posts, high enough for a man to reach with a pole the length of 8–10 ft. Contestants worked in pairs. One pushed the other in a wheelbarrow between the two posts, and the man sitting in the barrow had to try to get his pole through the hole in the board without upsetting the bucket. It rarely happened, and the delighted crowd could rely on yet another ducking. The pole was usually an old sounding-rod used for testing the depth of the water, when tacking in the Humber. Keelmen were very thrifty.

Another attraction was a second greasy pole, this time an upright one, which competitors had to climb in order to seize the flag at the top, and a very difficult, slithering and greasy feat it was. Most men managed to get near the top, then came sliding down the 18 ft pole with a great wallop.

The flat cycle-races drew good entries, and there were usually four or six heats for each event, and very exciting they were.

I sold programmes for both the land and the water sports. They cost 3d each, and I was paid 3d a dozen for selling them—it was slave labour!

The cycle races completed the week's programme, except for those who got drunk. The last night of the Fair was considered to be the night when most of the men and some young lads went on the binge, and although the police took the worst offenders to the police station, they rarely charged any of them. After all it was Fair Week, and it came round but once a year. Next day all would be quiet again, and the keels would slip off one by one. It was back to work for them and for me.

I had found a job in a bakehouse at the corner of the Green and Top Street—now called King Street. It was owned by a widow who provided me with a white jacket, and a bicycle with bread baskets lined and covered with white linen. I worked from eight o'clock in the morning until five at night for six days a week, and earned 5s. My main job was delivering orders, as I was too young to work in the bakehouse, although I often did. If an inspector came in, I had to pretend that I had just gone in for a warm. I once delivered a small Hovis costing 6d to a woman who lived half a mile away. She rang up for it and I had to cycle all that way with one small loaf.

Twice a week I had to deliver bread to the workhouse, where tramps could stay for one night and a meal. They had to work in return, chopping wood and carrying coal into the different rooms. They generally left after breakfast to tramp to the next workhouse.

Old people who had no means of support also lived there. They were always called the 'paupers'. They had to do most of the work, such as washing, cleaning, gardening and looking after those who were beyond working. If they could stand up at all, they had to work, and if they could sit down they had to sew and darn and mend. It was a hard life for old people, especially if they had a bad master who was afraid that the Board of Guardians would grumble because the workhouse was costing too much to run. I felt sorry for the old folks, and made up my mind that I for one would never end up in the workhouse.

After I had been at the bakery a week the widow asked if I would like to take the handcart out on Friday and Saturday afternoons to sell bread and pastry on my own. Of course I wanted to do this, and made 5s the first day, and 7s the second. The widow was so pleased that she gave me 2s extra and a bag of buns. Soon I was making 15s–£1 a day, so she doubled my wages. On Good Friday morning I delivered the Hot Cross Buns straight out of the oven. They were very good.

Ashore

I liked to watch the baker at work. He had to get up at 4 a.m. to light the fire for the big brick oven, which burnt gas coke and had to be glowing red before any bread was put in. He kneaded the dough in a wooden trough, first with a paddle and then with his hands. The loaves he made, called quartern loaves, were larger than the ones we have today. He would tear off two pieces of dough and roll them, two at a time, one in each hand. He also made Hovis loaves and milk loaves which were oval with a plait on the top. I helped him by taking the bread out of the tins with an oven cloth made of harden—a coarse cloth made from the refuse of 'hards' of flax and hemp—and cleaning and greasing the tins for the next batch.

He baked buns too: fairy buns and queen cakes, as well as currant slices and jam pies. My favourites were the Swiss rolls. He always made one big one, then cut it in half and trimmed off the edges. He and I ate the ends while they were still warm, and we argued about which end had the most jam. He also made wedding cakes, and was very good at icing them.

When I had finished my day and had my tea, I liked to go to Bellamy's farm, just across the street, where I helped the yardman to milk the cows by chaining them up and giving them their fodder. I also fed the bull and the boar which were kept in the fold yard. The bull followed me about when I had the bucket on my shoulder, and though big, it was quiet, not at all like the boar, which was a bad 'un. He once knocked me and two buckets of pig swill flying all over the yard, after which I always chased him into a stall and put the swill in his trough. On another occasion he chased the farmer and ripped his trousers with his tusks, where-upon the farmer chained him down and chiselled off the sharp ends of those tusks. The boar squealed but the farmer was stone deaf.

At haymaking and harvesting, the woman of the farm asked me to take the men their sandwiches and a drink. I went to the fields where they were working and after their meal (usually thick cheese sandwiches and bottles of beer) I was given a sandwich and a bottle of pop. I never wanted anything else to eat that night, as the sandwiches were one and a half inches thick.

Sometimes the farmer asked me to take a big ginger mare, pulling a water barrel to the pump at the corner of Ellison Street, fill the barrel and water the bullocks in their field. When I sat on the back of that great Shire mare, I nearly split in two, and *it* always took *me*, not the other way round. It was a lovely creature, almost human, and weighed nearly a ton. She had a beautiful foal that summer.

5 *Plater's apprentice*

I soon realized that the job in the baker's would not lead anywhere, so I told my parents I would like to change it. My father had a sister who lived in Hull, and one day she and her husband came to Thorne to visit us and my father told him I was looking for a better job. There was nothing for me in Thorne, so uncle suggested that I go to live in Hull with him and his wife. He had a brother who was a plater in a shipyard, and who might be able to get me work there, as it was wartime, and most of the young men had gone to France. So on 27 March 1915 I packed my things and went to work in Earle's shipbuilding yard, all set and independent from then on. I was fifteen years old.

I had always liked Hull. It was a clean city with plenty of parks and a seven-mile front along the river Humber, split in two by the river Hull, which was crossed by seven bridges. The seventh was a toll-bridge: ½d for pedestrians and 1d for a horse and cart. The city looks today very much as it did then. The layout is the same, although it was badly bombed during the Second World War. One dock has been filled in, the Queen's Dock, right in the centre of the city. It used to be known as the Old Dock, and now it is Queen's Gardens, with a fountain in the middle and paths that go up and down almost as much as the water used to.

Of course I knew the dockland well from my keeling days, and Hull Pier too, where the sloops used to run twice weekly sailings to New Holland on the Lincolnshire side of the Humber. There was also a daily ferry service between Hull and Grimsby by small steamships plying from the mouth of the river Hull near the pier. It still runs, and will run until they build the Humber Bridge.

I remember the electric trams with open tops and driving platforms, and the waggonettes licensed by the Council. Their drivers all wore a number on a metal disk. The trams stopped running at 10 p.m. but the waggonettes ran as long as they had passengers. They all started from the centre of the city, and the fare was ½d or 1d, depending on how far you wanted to go.

Hull is the only city I remember with a signal box, signals and a signalman in the main street. They were at the corner of Midland Street and Anlaby Road, and they controlled the trams and worked the points.

I can remember the present Guildhall being built, and also the General Post Office. I could always find my way about Hull, and still say you can't get lost there as each main road leads to the centre. In several places there were monuments and fountains in the middle of crossroads, but these have been removed for modern traffic.

I can remember Pickering Park and the Maritime Museum being built, and also Pickering Church, on land given by Sir Christopher Pickering, owner of the fleet of trawlers. Most of the land on which East Park stands was given by J. R. Ferens, the chairman of Reckitt's.

My uncle's house was in Balfour Street, only ten minutes' walk from the shipyard, and I started as marking-off boy with his brother Dave. My wage was 15s a week, less 2d for the unemployment stamp, and I paid my aunt 12s a week for board and lodging.

The yard was in East Hull, on the river Humber, and it looked a very big place to me on my first day at work. It employed between 3,000 and 4,000 men and boys and was a complete shipyard, making the ships, boilers and engines, and doing joinery and electrical work all within the same boundary fence. It could have four ships all being built at once. There were two modern slipways and two mud docks for fitting out ships after they had been launched. It must have been at least 500 yds square, with one side facing the river Humber.

To me, accustomed to the quiet of the canals and rivers, the noise was at first unbearable, and my head was buzzing long before the end of the first day. But I learnt to work in it, to shut out the noise and concentrate on the work I was doing. All shipyard men have to be able to think despite noise.

87

Plater's apprentice

All the ships made then were painted red at first, then when ready for sailing they were camouflaged with different colours. The smell of fresh paint was the first to hit me, but I soon discovered that steel has a smell of its own too. These two, combined with the smell of the river and of the rivet-heating fires and furnaces, make up the shipyard smell.

Most of the men dressed in moleskin trousers and jackets. Overalls were not in use, and the foremen all wore billycock hats and navy blue suits. This was a kind of uniform, and I believe it is still found in North Country and Scottish yards.

My first day at work was much easier than I had expected. All I did was to carry a pot of white paint and a paint-brush around after the plater, who chalked numbers on the pieces, or 'plates', of steel which had to come off a ship under repair. I then painted over his chalkmarks. The plater was on lieu rate, which was an average of what he could earn if he was on piecework, and it was paid on jobs which could not be worked on piecework. In Hull it was generally paid for repairing boats, as it was almost impossible to get continuity in work of that kind.

Some platers worked for a basic rate which was low and usually refused by good platers. Some inland plating shops engaged on constructional work, not shipbuilding, worked on time and a quarter of the basic rate, and if the foreman thought any particular plater was worth more, he could get time and a half, but he had to be the foreman's blue-eyed boy.

I stayed with that first plater, Dave Farrar, for about a month, then he left the yard and I was placed with another plater who was on piecework. He would put the wooden template on the steel plate and leave me to mark the holes for the rivets. This was done with a brass peg made of brass or copper tube the exact size of the holes to be punched in the plate later.

He would be talking to somebody all the time I was working, and if I had not finished when he came back, he would give me an almighty clout behind the ear. At the end of a week with him I was ready to pack up and go home, but on the Friday he said I had done well and gave me 2s pocket money. He said I was to take no notice of what he said, or of his smacks, which were not so hard. He gave me that 2s all the time I was with him. I learnt later that he was known as Mad Jack.

He was $14\frac{1}{2}$ st of bone and muscle, a rugby footballer and as strong as an ox. He was of Scottish descent, though born in England. He was all right as long as I got on with my work, and got on fast, and he told the foreman I was the best lad he'd ever had, after which the foreman took a keen interest in me. I was with Mad Jack for about six months.

We started work at 6 a.m. with half an hour for breakfast, an hour for dinner, and we finished at 5 p.m. Every morning we went to the time office to draw our boards. These boards were made of wood, about 2 in × 3 in and we had our works number burnt in the top. We had to wet them, rub them over with white chalk, then during the day write details of our work on them with pencil. At night we threw them into a basket so that the office staff could note what we had been doing. The next day we picked up a second board. The two were always alternating.

We were allowed seven minutes a day lavatory time, and I don't know what happened if anyone took longer. I suppose he had the amount deducted from his wages. To make sure you had the seven minutes and no more, you had to hand your timeboard to a man in the office at the latrines. He booked your number and your times, and gave you a key to one of the toilets. When you handed the key back he returned your timeboard.

Funnily enough, in certain parts of the yard like the joiners' shop, the boilers' shop and the engineering shop, there were more latrines with no officials in attendance. Not unnaturally most of us went to these when we had to.

On Saturdays we worked from 6 a.m. to 12 noon—fifty-three hours a week. All pieceworkers were allowed a fifteen minute break every morning, and we all took advantage of it. What amazed me was that after every holiday all the men in the boiler-makers' union would go to work, stand and talk for about an hour, and then go home. It was a tradition among boilermakers.

They had another tradition too. If a man was killed in the yard, all the workers went home for the rest of the day, and if he was a plater, all the platers would have the day off to follow his funeral and collect for his widow. An average collection was £15.

During the seven years I was at Earle's shipyard, there were six men killed. The first fell 60 ft and broke his neck, and the second was attending a crane as a slinger when the crane jib hit an overhead cast-iron windpipe, which broke and fell on him. Another was killed by a bar which came unfastened from a crane and buried itself in his head. It took two men to get it out. These three at least, would not have died under present-day safety precautions.

There were plenty of odd accidents too, such as burns and broken arms and legs, but they were everyday occurrences. Cuts and bruises, and bits of steel in the hands were not even considered worth a visit to the First Aid Post.

By the time I was sixteen my wages had gone up to 18s a week, and we were working a good bit of overtime. I gave my aunt another 2s a week, as my uncle's wages as a railway goods checker did not amount to much.

Then the yard got some minesweepers to build, and the foreman asked me if I would go on the countersinking machine to help the firm out. It was really a man's work, paid as piecework, and they couldn't afford a man's wage. I did not want to take it on, as I knew I should not be learning anything, and it was hard work, but the foreman said he would see I did not lose by it, so I agreed.

It was killing work. By the end of the day my arms felt as if they were dropping off, and we were working until seven o'clock three nights a week. Countersinking was the process of putting a bevel on the holes in the plates, so that the rivets got a good hold and helped to make the ship watertight. The machine had a long arm which I had to lift up and then press, so that the tool on the other end dropped into the hole and cut out the metal. It was designed for a man, and I was only 5 ft 4½ in tall, so I had to be always reaching up. In addition, I only weighed 8½ st, which meant that I had to press harder to get the amount of countersink required. It was hard on the hands and the arms, and if I touched the tool it was so hot that I continually got huge blisters. No man stuck it for long, and after a fortnight I asked the foreman to take me off, as it was much harder than marking off, yet the wages were just the same. He asked me whether I would stick it if he could get me a bit more money, but I was not keen. He even took me to the office to arrange an increase in pay, but the pay clerk said it was impossible, as I was only sixteen. The foreman pointed out that I was doing a man's work, and that there was a war on. They would be in a real fix if I came off the machine, so to get over the problem they agreed to give me a 2s a week bonus, making my pay 20s.

After another fortnight my uncle told me to tell the foreman that the work was too hard for a boy. I even used to fall asleep as I was having my tea. I delivered my message, and the foreman and the countersinker had a chat, as a result of which the countersinker offered me 2s a week out of his own pocket if I would stay with him, but I said it was not the extra money I wanted. The fact was that I was absolutely worn out. The foreman took me into his office and asked me about my life, how I was living, where my parents were, and what ambitions I had. I told him I wanted to be a plater, but realized that since I had no relations in the yard I had very little chance of becoming one.

To this he replied, 'Well, we're in a real hole if you come off the machine. You're a good timekeeper, and a very good worker. If you stick to the machine until the minesweepers are finished, I'll see you get an apprenticeship to a plater—no matter what the other platers say.' I wanted that more than anything else, but I couldn't really believe it would happen. However, he said I could rely on him, so I took his word for it.

He was a Londoner, about thirty-seven years old and 14 st. He was part of the stern squad who built the aft end of ships: the most difficult part to do, as the plates have to be heated in a furnace and shaped while hot. It was a job most platers, including me, dodged in later life. I could never stand the heat.

He was always cheerful, and called me Sunny Jim, whilst the rest of the yard called me Smiler Fletcher. When, later on, some platers complained about my apprenticeship, he told them I had earned it by hard work and good timekeeping, and as he was well liked by the men, no more was said.

That foreman looked after me like a father. I stayed on the countersinker for four months, and on the day the minesweepers were finished he told me to go to his office the following morning at nine o'clock. I was there prompt. He took me to the manager and explained the position and the promise he had made me, and asked for me to be signed on then and there as an apprentice plater. The manager said that after all he had heard he thought I had earned the privilege, so without any further waiting I was signed on. It was 7 February 1916.

When I told my uncle I was an apprentice he refused to believe me, saying that only platers' sons got apprenticeships; but I had the signed agreement to prove it. Still unconvinced, he went along to the yard to see if the foreman was having me on a string. The foreman told him that he had no doubts that I would make a good plater, or he would not have gone to so much trouble on my behalf. I did not know this until long after the event, but my father was very pleased, and as for me, I was on top of the world.

The apprenticeship was for five years, and I was sixteen and a half years old. My first week's earnings were £1 0s 3d, so I began to pay my aunt 16s a week. I did not smoke or drink, so I was well away, and I started to put money in the bank for when we had short weeks. Holidays were not paid, so every Easter, Whitsuntide and Christmas we lost two and a half days' pay.

I wanted to be a plater because they were the men who actually made the ships. They did all the steelwork except for the boilers and the engines and I thought that their work was the most interesting of all. A plater had to know how to read a blueprint or drawing of a ship and from it make wooden patterns or templates for the steel. He made these templates from lathes about $\frac{1}{4}$ in thick and 3, 4 or 5 in wide according to which part of the ship he was making. They were only made for half the ship, either the port or starboard side and then turned over to do the other half, for all ships were made from the centre line outwards.

When a template for the shell plates or skin of the ship, for instance, was ready the plater who was the 'marker-off' took his marker boy to the ship, which was already framed out on the building berth, and clipped the template into the position marked on the blueprint. The boy then marked through the holes in the frames on to the template with a mixture of whitening and water (not paint), so that the marks could be rubbed off and the template used again for another ship.

The 'marker-off' then laid the template on the steel plate and the holes for the rivets were marked off with a short brass or copper tube called a 'marking peg'. This was dipped in white paint and pressed on the plates, making a ring of paint to show the plater 'puncher' where to punch the holes. That's what I had done for Mad Jack who was a 'marker-off'. Marking off had to be accurate as the hole in the plate and the frames had to match exactly so that they could be riveted together. If they didn't the steel was wasted and so was a lot of money and time.

The plate then went to the plater who was the 'puncher' and he had to make the holes for the rivets in a punching press, powered by an electric motor on a belt. On the other side of this machine were the shears and the same plate was 'sheared', that is, cut to the size and shape required. Mistakes here were just as costly.

If the plate had to be made watertight it was then taken to my old friend the countersinking machine, where a bevel was put on the holes in the plates. The man operating the machine was not a plater but he was semi-skilled, as were all the helpers who helped the platers to move the plates about and operate the machinery. Each plater in Earle's had at least one helper and sometimes as many as five or even eight, and 'platers' helping' was almost a trade in itself.

After countersinking, the shell plates had to be 'scarphed' and 'planed' in machines operated by more semi-skilled men. The outside plate or strake had to be smoothed or planed where it lapped over the next plate, so that the ship had a good line, and the inside plates were scarphed or tapered where they overlapped so that the plates lay smoothly with no rough edges.

When the plates were ready, the plater who was 'erecting' went to the ship with some strips of iron which he hammered or bent to the shape required, then he rolled the plate cold to the same shape as the iron strips, called 'gauges', in a set of rollers. He and his helpers then took the plate to the ship and by means of winches and blocks and wires erected or hung up the plate into the position marked on the blueprint and bolted it up ready for riveting.

Plating, then, was basically marking off, punching and shearing and erecting. I wanted to be a 'marker-off' but at first I was put under a chargehand plater along with another youth, since they always worked two apprentices together, and always on piecework. The first thing the chargehand did was to take us into the office, give us a drawing-office blueprint, and tell us to make some bulkhead brackets.

Bulkheads are the steel watertight divisions across the ship which divide the holds from the engine and boiler rooms. The other lad didn't even know what part of the ship they went in, since he had been working with a plater who did most of the work himself, so he didn't know a bulkhead from a bracket. This was where I reaped the benefit of working with Mad Jack, for he had shown me how to read a drawing.

We were rather slow at first, and the other lad was not used to hard work, so I had to push him on. He was living at home with his parents, and wasn't bothered about earning money, whereas I was in lodgings and had to earn to pay my way. He could not even make out the piecework bill, so I had to do it. This was a type-written sheet we got from the chargehand. On a Wednesday morning we had to put down everything we had done in the week, and the chargehand had to see that we had really done the work we had booked. Then he handed it in to the piecework office. On the Saturday at nine o'clock we had to go to the office for a yellow sheet which listed the prices for all the jobs we had done during the past week together with our stoppages and our net wage. This had to be shared equally between us. I had to get the money, as my partner would not go for it. Then I had to share it out. I was getting a bit tired of doing all the work for both of us.

One morning the foreman called me into his office and asked me what was wrong. He had been watching me and thought I was not happy. I told him frankly that I had to earn a living, and that my partner was not bothered. He had started going to dances and coming to work half asleep. The foreman said he had noticed what was happening, and had been waiting for me to go to him. He told me again that if ever I needed advice I must ask him, and he ended by suggesting that I went with his own son, who was punching and erecting, and who had begun his apprenticeship six months before me.

My only fear was that I might not get enough experience at marking off, as his son would be doing this, and it was the most important part of plating, but he said he would see to it that I became a good all-round plater. Knowing by then that I could rely on his word, I agreed. He got me three good plater's helpers, all old enough to be my father. One was called the leading hand. He got 3s a week extra for this, and he was the best helper I ever had. He could do the rig for erecting almost anything, and I learnt a great deal from him. He was another with a nickname: Cock Fewster. If you called him Arthur, he didn't know who you were speaking to.

We were a hard-working team, and we got bigger and better jobs as the war went on, for platers were scarce, and we were given work we should never have had in peacetime. My wages for 1916 came to £60 4s 2d and this included eleven months as an apprentice.

There were two brothers in the yard who specialized in making bulkheads. They were very good platers, and when their puncher was off work, or 'lost a quarter', they would come for me to take his place, and the foreman let me go on condition that they paid me the same as their regular puncher, 2s 6d an hour. When this happened the foreman's son had to take my helpers and keep going on his own until the puncher came back.

If a man 'lost a quarter' it meant he had gone to work at 9 a.m. instead of 6 a.m., and so lost a quarter of a day's pay. If this happened too often, it meant dismissal in peacetime, but in wartime you were sent before a tribunal which could pack you off into the armed forces for not pulling your weight.

Punching was putting the rivet holes into the steel plates with a punching and shearing machine. A die the size of the hole to be punched was fixed into the machine, and a punch, slightly smaller, was fixed on the arm above. The machine worked at the rate of thirty-two a minute, and the plater-puncher and his helpers had to move the plate so that the holes, marked in white paint, were directly under the punch.

Then another plater who did all the casings and superstructure asked me to punch for him so I suggested to my mate, the other apprentice, that we pooled our extra earnings and shared them equally. The foreman did not agree, and said I should keep all that I earned punching myself, but I argued that this was not fair to my mate, who was, of course, the foreman's son. He had, I knew, to pay board at home, as his father believed in making him stand on his own feet. I got my way and the arrangement worked very well. Sometimes he got work for other platers at 2s 6d an hour, and we shared that. His name was Ted Austin and he was bigger than I was, well built, and better educated. He was a nice lad then, and is just as nice a man now, sixty years later.

Once the brothers had the job of strengthening two shallow-draught vessels called monitors. Because they could get in and out of the dock at any time, high or low tide, it had been decided to put guns on them for shooting zeppelins. We had destroyers with guns of course, but they could only fire in the river and were dependent upon tides to get out of the docks. The guns on these monitors, the *Crocus* and the *Cricket*, kept the zeppelins out of range all right but shook so badly whenever they fired that they were dangerous to be on. It was our job to strengthen them enough to carry their anti-aircraft guns with safety.

The foreman could not spare a plater to help the brothers but offered them the pick of the apprentices, twenty-three of us, and they chose me. The work lasted about three months, and the foreman refused point blank to let me share the money I made, which was 3s 6d an hour. It was hard work, but invaluable experience, as the platers had to design and make the job on their own without any drawings to guide them, but I enjoyed it. When it was finished I went to the foreman and said, 'What happens now?' He told me not to be so bloody daft, but to get back to where I was before. His son was as pleased as I was, as he did not like being in charge of three helpers, and was shy of telling them what to do. One of them had taken a dislike to him and had been a bit awkward, but soon everything was ticking over fine again.

It was about this time that we started to work on repairs, for which we were paid by a method called 'Grip Work', as piecework rates were not allowed for repair work. The foreman would come along and say, 'I've got a job here, and I can give you all night'; or perhaps 'I've got a job here and you can have till ten o'clock to do it.' It then became a question of bargaining until an agreement over a price was reached. These jobs were generally done at night, or at weekends, as we were so busy building new ships during the day.

Once, they wanted to put guns on a merchant ship to fight off submarines. It was agreed that two platers, three helpers and a marking boy should get all-night pay to make a complete gun-stand ready for riveting. We could, by working hard, finish one about midnight, which meant we earned a little more than time and a half, and also were able to get some sleep before the next day's work. Without the Grip system, we should have had to stay until 5 a.m. This method cut down the time required to repair ships by a considerable amount, and was liked by the firm as well as by the men. In some cases it is still used, but often unfairly in slack times.

The guns on the merchant ships were mounted on the stern deck, and in some cases it was necessary to remove a deckhouse. If this was in good condition it was stored ready to go back after the war. If not, it went for scrap iron, which was very scarce.

I once started on a minelayer which had been hit by a torpedo and was urgently needed. I began work at 6 a.m. on Monday and

19. Thorne Travis Charity School (author arrowed)

20. Albert Dock, Hull

21. The 'old harbour', Hull

22. Rank's flour mill near the entrance
to Victoria Dock on the river Hull

23. The author's father, 'Young Jim',
with a friend

worked until 10 p.m. Starting again at 6 a.m. Tuesday, I worked through all night until 5 a.m. On Wednesday it was 6 a.m. until 10 p.m.; on Thursday 6 a.m. until 5 a.m.; on Friday 6 a.m. until 10 p.m. and on Saturday 6 a.m. until 4 p.m., when the job was finished at last. We were asleep as we walked about. It was a ridiculous arrangement, since no man can work such long hours and continue to give of his best. The only good thing about it was the pay. This was not piecework. We called it 'lieu rate' or 'on the nod', an average per hour of our piecework earnings.

I did not care much for repair work, as it was just a question of putting something back as it was before. I preferred building new ships, where new ideas were being tried out, and where, when a ship was finished, you could look at it and say, 'I helped to create that.'

My most exciting job was for the Admiralty, which sent us drawings and templates for some false whaleback. Whaleback is the curved covering over the foredeck of a trawler and is part of the original construction of the vessel. The whaleback we had to build was false whaleback because it had to be made on its own and then welded to the vessel concerned. We had no idea what that vessel would be. We built the whaleback in a shed and folded it together ready for riveting. Sometime afterwards we had to take it to pieces again, load these on lorries and take them to King George Dock. We were given a pass to go on board the vessel and put up the whaleback, and when we reached the dock I could hardly believe my eyes. A steam submarine was waiting for us. She was the K5, and we did the whaleback not only for her, but for the K10 as well. Everybody in the yard wanted to see them, as until then it had been considered impossible to build such vessels.

The whaleback was meant to give them greater buoyancy, as they had a tendency to dive too steeply. It fitted on the fore end of the submarine, and was not a great success. Neither were the submarines, most of which were lost, and not through enemy action. They were much bigger than present-day submarines, and were more like destroyers, with two funnels and ventilators. These collapsed, and watertight covers worked by electricity covered the openings. When the vessel dived, the heat in the boiler room had to stay there until it surfaced again. The snorkel had not yet been invented. The electricity was stored in large batteries which gave off dangerous fumes if they ever got wet.

ALH—G

Our next job was to make two minelayers in a hurry, and we had to stop all other building. There were so many men on these ships that if you put a hand on the deck somebody trod on it. It was murder! Everybody got in everybody else's way, nobody could get on with the work in a reasonable manner, and no end of time was wasted. It was all very silly.

Then we got the cruiser *Albion* to repair. She was too big to get into Hull, and stayed anchored in the river off Immingham. We were taken to her down the Humber on a tug called the *Elsa Parkiss*, and we worked for thirty-six hours, and then had twenty-four off. This again was ridiculous, as no man could work efficiently for thirty-six hours at a stretch. It took nearly three months to finish the job. Some men used to be so sick on the tug going down the river that they were no good for work when they finally got there. I never knew who was responsible for the planning, but he can hardly have been a practical man.

Next there were tugs to be built for the river Thames, and we apprentices built them entirely alone.

During the war the finer points of shipbuilding were neglected for speed and utility. Ships known as standard ships were built with no fancy work, just plain cargo carriers. They were designed for quick construction, and were made in three sizes. The idea was that one drawing would serve for all the shipyards in the country, and that parts made in one yard would fit a ship being built in another. The position in shipping was becoming so bad because of the U-boats that men who had any skill at all in shipbuilding were being sent back from the trenches still covered in French mud. They were allowed twenty-four hours' leave, then had to be at work. We had several of them, some of whom had been gassed and were in a very poor condition.

Another interesting job I was given was that of taking the saloon skylights off the paddle ferry-boats *Killingholme* and *Brocklesby*, and converting them to carry three seaplanes, which went on the decks and on the top of the saloon. They were lifted off with a derrick and placed on the water. It was their duty to patrol the east coast spotting submarines. The *Brocklesby* later struck a mine with her paddle, but managed to beach, and after being patched up she came back to the yard, and I was one of the gang used to repair her.

We were building and repairing as fast as we could. I was once loaned out to a plater who was repairing a destroyer. He had to make a handrail round the wheelhouse, and when it was finished we took it to the ship, which was in the dock, and laid it on the stanchions ready for drilling. One of the officers promptly came on deck, leaned on it, and into the dock went officer and rail together. Of course we laughed—which didn't please the officer.

I worked on several destroyers, and also on the cruiser *St George*, one of two built at the yard before my time—the other being the *Endymion*. I helped to repair the cruiser *Chester*, on which the gunner-boy Jack Cornwell won his VC by staying at his station in the gun-turret after all the gun-crew had been killed. She was like a colander, with holes all over her from really big shells. How anybody lived to get back to England I don't know.

During my time in the yard we built the biggest ship ever commissioned there. She was the *Condesa*, built for Houlder Brothers, the shipowners. She was a twin-screw ship, in other words she had two propellers. Her engines were quadruple expansion, four-cylinder marine engines, served by five marine boilers of high-pressure working. She was refrigerated throughout and had 94 miles of pipes in her for freezing, and tons of broken cork for insulation. She had nine decks, and meat was hung beneath each deck. She was said to be worth £1 million with her cargo, a tidy sum in those days, but she was lost by enemy action on her first voyage when she was almost home.

I had some good jobs when I was working on her. I once walked across one of her deck beams 3½ in wide and 62 ft across. It was swaying a little when I got to the middle, and the foreman said his heart was in his mouth. I said, 'That makes two of us!' He also said that if I did it again he would have me sacked. That deck beam was 60 ft high!

Two destroyers of M Class 2, the *Manley* and the *Morris*, then came in for repairs. They had three turbines: two for going ahead and one for going astern.

Next we had a ship with a cargo of oranges which had struck a mine just off the Humber, and it took six tugs to get her into the yard, four of them pumping and two towing. They got her on to the mud, where she soon settled down, but our longest gangway was too short to reach her, so we had to sling it with wires, and use planks to make up the gap. Three of the crew had been killed and many others were taken to hospital. The oranges had helped to keep her afloat—and lovely oranges they were too.

Although other ships that had been struck by mines came into the yard, I worked on only one that had been torpedoed. Generally when a ship was struck by a torpedo, that was the end of it. If it did not sink straight away, the U-boat would shell it until it did, since the whole idea was to sink as many ships as possible. Some submarines picked up the crews if they could, and transferred them to prison ships.

One of the most moving scenes I witnessed was the funeral procession of fourteen coffins, covered with Union Jacks, each on a gun carriage pulled by sailors, from the pier at Hull. All the dead were from one of our submarines sunk off the coast of Norway. Their bodies had been recovered and brought to us by the Norwegians. All the Naval top brass and Army generals were there, and we were allowed time off to go and watch the ceremony. It was a lovely day. The route was lined by soldiers standing with arms reversed, and there were crowds of people standing in the bright sunshine to pay their respects.

I well remember the first time the zeppelins bombed Hull. I woke to find my bedroom lit up from a fire started by a bomb in a woodyard. People were running about in their nightclothes, more surprised than panic-stricken, as there had been no warning buzzer. Most of the harm done was caused by fire. During one raid bombs were dropped in Queen's Street in the town, and damaged buildings on both sides of the road as well as setting fire to a clothing and general stores, which was burnt to the ground. After this raid, warnings were always given, and many people would run for the parks or open spaces, taking their children and blankets with them.

We never heard the zeppelins approaching. They switched off their engines and drifted in on the wind like great grey ghosts. Then they dropped their bombs, switched on their engines, and were full speed away. For a time we had no guns which could reach them, but towards the end of the war we had better planes, and I remember how elated we all were when a zeppelin was finally set on fire by 'one of ours'.

There was a great deal of anti-German feeling, and a number of German pork butchers' shops were broken into and looted. This was in spite of the fact that the pork butcher on Holderness

Road had fed almost a whole street during the dock strike in 1912. One German who had been naturalized, and whose sons, born in Britain, were serving in the British Army, was interned for his own protection. The shop on Hedon Road where my parents had bought home-cured hams was raided, and the police had to rescue the butcher and his family. The mob threw all his furniture, including a piano, from the upstairs window, then they broke the piano to pieces in the street. This was the work of hooligans and thieves, since the shop was stripped bare.

Whilst I was living at my aunt's I had hot bread cakes and bacon for breakfast every morning. She used to make the dough for the cakes the night before. She had a credit account at a shop which sold almost everything, and she took me there to be measured for my first suit. First I got the coat and waistcoat in navy blue serge, for which I paid 1s a week, and when they were paid for I got the trousers, and after that a pair of best boots. I was a proper dandy!

I used to go to Sherburn Picture House, where for 2½d I saw Pearl White in a serial on Mondays, Tuesdays or Wednesdays, and Elmo Lincoln in another on Thursdays, Fridays or Saturdays. Sometimes I bought a fish-and-chip supper for 1½d, a penny fish and a ha'pennyworth of chips, and finished off with a bottle of pop for 1d. I could enjoy this high living twice a week for 10d.

My uncle took me to see Hull Kingston Rovers at Craven Park playing Northern Rugby Union football, now Rugby League. I was so excited about the game that I asked if boys played it, and when I heard that they did, it took me less than a week to sign on with Barnsley United in the Hull and District Junior League. I played for five years, mainly with a team called Norwood. I was the only non-Catholic in the team of eighteen players—thirteen in the team and five reserves. We stripped at the Conservative Club on Holderness Road, and went to the various grounds by horse waggonette, wearing our overcoats over our strip, which was dark green, with one horizontal pale green stripe, and a light green shamrock on the left breast.

I paid 1s a week to the Football Club, so I always had 1s left, which I saved so that I could occasionally go home for the weekend. To get to Thorne I had to catch an electric tram on Holderness Road to Paragon Station, and a train to Thorne North Station. I usually spent the weekend meeting old schoolmates, playing the part of a man about town, or visiting relatives, working on the farm, and on Saturday night going to the cinema yet again. As I did not get to Thorne until about four o'clock on the Saturday, and left again at 5.30 on the Sunday, there was never much time to spare.

I never really lost contact with the river Humber, as all the ships we built were launched into it. Besides Cock Fewster, my leading helper had a trawler's boat which he had bought second-hand and was converting for fishing and shrimping and I helped him all I could. She was tarred black with grey top work, and had small cabins which would sleep two, and often did. She was a good sea boat, strong, and though not as fast as some, much safer.

For a time he kept the boat inside the conveyor jetty at Alexandra Dock, then when it became too difficult to get in and out, he moved it into the river Hull, where a few boats were anchored. Since he wasn't fishing for a living he didn't need a licence nor did he pay rent for the boat as river dues were charged only on cargoes carried. But he did have to register both the boat and himself with the River Board because it was wartime and all shipping had to be easily identifiable.

We went out every weekend when the tides were suitable and trawled for shrimps and fish with an 8 ft beam net. We had no motor, only sails and because we had so little power often cursed the *Duke of Clarence*, a steamship of the Associated Humber Lines. She sailed a regular service to the Continent from Riverside Quay and she was a bad ship for leaving a large backwash. All small boats and keels used to swear at her when she went down the Humber at speed because her wake could damage nets or even send small craft crashing into sandbanks. She went so fast that she was known to the stokers as a 'hellfire ship' or the 'stoker's nightmare' or the 'stoker's grave' and many other expressions, some of them unprintable. So our fishing trips were not without incident.

Once, when we had been out all night, we woke up to the sound of buzzers. A tug was towing a target along the river, and the Paull battery of guns was firing at full blast. Shells were flying all over us. Of course they were blank, but if one had fallen short and hit us, we should have sunk. We lost no time in getting out of the way!

Another time we got close to a cruiser which was anchored inside the boom, and a launch came out after us. We had great difficulty in convincing them that we were fishing not spying.

Our saddest encounter was when we saw a little boy waving a

towel from another boat. When we finally got to him, he told us that his father and eleven-year-old brother had been drowned, and that he was all by himself. He was only nine years old. I sailed his boat back to Hull about ten miles away, while my helper sailed our own boat. The little lad never spoke a word on that journey back. My helper, who knew his mother, took him home. The full story was that his father and brother had got into the small boat to try to turn the fishing net which had been forced the wrong way up by a strong tide. It was a manœuvre I had often been warned never to attempt. They should have hauled the net in and reshot it. The tide had capsized the boat on Holme Sand, just below Paull. Their bodies were picked up on the coast at Easington about three weeks later, within a day of each other and almost in the same place.

We went out ourselves one lovely Sunday morning, when suddenly it started to blow a gale and to rain very hard. We started back for Hull as quickly as we could. Some other fishermen were watching us from Alexandra Dock through glasses, and asked a tug to go out and fetch us in, but when they told the tug's captain who we were, he refused to go. 'Oh, those two will make it!' he said. He had a lot more faith than we had, though my early training with the keel came in very handy. My helper was sailing, and I was pumping hard, as we were taking so much water over the top, but luckily we had no leaks and got back without any help.

Sometimes if it was calm and there was not enough wind to tow the net, we would put the boat broadside to the tide and let it drift with the net. We never caught fish by this method, only shrimps, as we were not going very fast, and the fish could swim out of the net as fast as they swam in.

Another method used in calm weather was 'sweep netting'. One of us would get on a sandbank with two lines, one at the top of the net and one at the bottom. The bottom line was weighted with lead to keep it down. Then the other lad would get into a small dinghy, fasten the lines to it, and row in a small circle to the sands. We then pulled the lines tight to hold the fish in, hauled the net on to the sand and collected the fish—if there were any. On a warm day this was a very pleasant way of passing the time.

In winter, when the shrimps had gone, we tried 'long lining', for which we used two lines with sinkers on the bottom and floats on the top. Between the two we attached a long line with a hundred baited hooks. All the baits, mussels or herring, had to be tied to the hooks with horsehair, or the tide would have washed them off. We dropped one sinker and float, and as the boat was going at about 5 knots the line had to be coiled so that it did not foul. That was a work of art! We dropped anchor when we had played out the line, then dropped the other float and sinker. We could then have a sleep for about four hours until slack water, the change from ebb to tide. Then we would haul the line up. If our luck was in we could have as much as a stone of codling on the line. Of course there were times when we had nothing at all, but we enjoyed the trip.

When we caught shrimps, my job was to boil them whilst my mate put the net down to trawl for more and look after the boat. We had a little boiler aboard with a coal fire. I had made the stove at work. I washed and sorted the shrimps from the fish, and put about 2 lb in a net bag. When the water was boiling I dropped them in, waited until it boiled again, then put them in a riddle to dry. I had to keep at it until I had boiled the whole catch, and if, as sometimes happened, we had 2 st of shrimps, we were back in Hull before I had finished boiling. Then we would go alongside the mud-dredger at Alexandra Dock, and the watchmen would let us finish boiling in their galley. I used to take 2 or 3 lb home with me, and my mate would take the rest to his pub and sell them at 6d a pint-glassful. The landlord always asked him to put plenty of salt in them, though they were salty already, since we had boiled them in salt river water, which we skimmed, and to which we added the salt that was used for salting cod and kippers. It looked like white peas!

The fish we caught were usually codling and whiting, small and sweet, with hardly any bones. If we ever caught smelt or soles, my mate would sell them, and could get 3s a pound for smelt, and 3s a pair for sole, and he spent the money on replacing sails, ropes and nets. We always caught sole in pairs, since they swam in pairs. Sometimes we caught a trout or a small plaice, and once we caught a lamprey eel.

At one time there were two or three men at Paull who made their living from fishing and shrimping but there aren't any today. Most of the shrimps and fish have gone from the Humber— probably because of the oil from the ships and barges.

Plater's apprentice

In 1917 my parents came to live in Hull as my father had taken a job on the lighters. Naturally I went to live with them, paying £1 a week for my board out of the £1 1s 10d I earned.

It was not long after my seventeenth birthday that I started to be interested in girls. A group of us apprentices went about together, but not as a gang causing trouble or doing damage. We played rugby together and went out with the same group of girls, meeting them inside the pictures, each paying for ourselves—2½d. We would even go to the park and play skipping or rounders and we eventually split into three couples. The girl I was taking out then left Hull, so that put an end to my romance.

Then one of the boys in the group had an abscess on his neck, and after taking him to hospital I had to go to his girlfriend, a fresh-faced girl with brown ringlets and sparkling hazel eyes, and explain why he could not come. Her name was Elizabeth Scott and I asked her if she would go to the pictures with me instead, and from then on we were a twosome. So, by acting as a stand-in, I acquired a wife.

Her father was a 'holder-up' in a shipyard, though it was not the one in which I worked. The holder was the man who worked inside the ship, putting the hot rivets into the holes and holding a large hammer on them while the two riveters outside knocked them down with two smaller hammers. My father-in-law weighed between 15 and 16 st, and stood about 6 ft: a real Viking, with very fair hair and deep blue eyes. He always wore his hair cut short with a fringe at the front, and had a moustache. His skin was fair and his hands were like ham-shanks. He was a very handy man, and a good woodworker who had built a small sailing boat by himself, and was then a partner in the building of a steel yacht. Everything he made was strong and built to last. I still have two pairs of steps he made in 1920, and though they are fifty-five years old, they are as good as the day he turned them out.

Liz and I, for I never called her Elizabeth, went to the theatre once or twice a week, sometimes to the Palace, where we would queue for an hour to get a seat, and where we saw some of the top stars in variety—Gertie Gitana, G. H. Elliot, Marie Lloyd, Hetty King, Florrie Ford, Jack Johnson, the boxer, and George Formby. At the Tivoli we saw Gracie Fields, Dickie Henderson and many others, and sometimes we went to the Alexandra Theatre and saw the Watson Mills Repertory Company, which used to come to

Hull for eight weeks at a time. Their repertoire included *The Murder in the Red Barn, The Man who Stayed at Home, Should a Woman Tell* and *The White Feathers*: melodramas all. For a change, we would try horror at the Grand Theatre—*The Silent House, Dracula, The Bat,* and as a complete contrast, *Charley's Aunt.* Once we even saw *Aïda.* We enjoyed the live theatre much more than the cinema.

Sometimes I went to the Empire to see boxing, but I went alone, as my girl did not like it, and there I saw Con O'Kelly, Gus Platts, Freddie Fox and others including Phil Scott, Benyon and a keelman called Dick Gillyon.

Liz had relations in Goole, and one Sunday we took a river trip there on the paddle-steamer *Atlanta,* but somehow or other we missed it when it was time to come back. We had to stay the night with her relations and come back by train on Monday morning. I managed to get to work for 9 a.m. but I got a telling-off from her mother for missing the boat. My friend and his girl-friend were with us. The girls were wearing big pink picture hats which got covered with smuts from the funnel of the boat. They were quite spoilt, so we were in trouble again.

These trips were run from the pier every Sunday in the summer. On an earlier trip before the Armistice we went across on the Humber ferry to New Holland and caught a tram from there to Cleethorpes. We were due back in Hull at 9.30 p.m., but there was an air-raid alarm, and the train had to stop until the all-clear sounded. It was 1.30 before we got home, since we had to walk from Hull Pier, which took us three-quarters of an hour, and we were both tired and hungry when we finally got back.

On some Sundays we cycled to Hornsea and Withernsea about 18 miles away, spent the day on the beach, then cycled back again.

The girls worked at a factory making clothing for the Army, and Liz was a machinist. I would leave work at five o'clock, dash home for my tea, and be at Hull Pier to meet her at six o'clock almost every night. Sometimes they had to work until eight o'clock, and then I would go to a shop near the factory and have a plate of bananas and custard at a little café, which also sold ice-cream, sarsaparilla, mineral waters and hot oxo in winter. It was kept by a Jew, a small slim man who had lived a long time in England, and always said he was an Englishman. He was about sixty, and had lost his wife some years before. He seemed to be a very lonely old man, and when I got to know him we played draughts together and had a chat even though he was old enough to be my grandfather. He liked me to go, as it was the only time he got a game, since none of his family could play. He died soon after the war ended.

There were quite a lot of Jews in Hull at that time, but never any anti-Jewish feeling that I knew of. In fact many Jews were well liked, and held office as councillors.

By 1918 my earnings had gone up to £111 14s 9d and we were still building standard ships. When one of these came for its engines and boilers, it was my job to take the casing top off to get them in, and then to replace the casing. This was called an *A* job.

The Armistice was signed on 11 November 1918. The war had ended at last. Everybody downed tools and went home to celebrate. People were dancing and singing in the streets and all over the place. Everybody was on top of the world except those who had lost sons, husbands or fathers. Peace came too late for them. At my girl's home it was very quiet. The youngest son had been killed in France, another was still there, and a third was a prisoner-of-war in Turkey. The last two had given the wrong age to get into the Army, and had joined up at seventeen. One of them had even had operations on both his legs so that he could get to France to fight. There were parties in the streets for the children, dancing and singing and fancy-dress parades, but there were many on-lookers with tears in their eyes.

Later we watched ships passing the yards bringing prisoners-of-war home from Germany, and we could hear the men singing as they came up the river, but they were too far off for us to shout or wave. They disembarked at Riverside Quay, and were put straight into trains to go to clearing stations or hospitals. None of them went straight home.

Peace came slowly at first. It seemed strange to see the streets lit up at night after four years of total darkness, but we were all happy except that in November overtime was reduced to a bare necessity, and in 1919 was stopped altogether, so my wages increased only slightly, totalling £118 4s 6d in that year.

The minefields which had been laid along the coast to protect our beaches from invasion were no longer necessary so the mines had to be removed quickly as some were breaking loose and becoming a danger to our shipping. At Earle's we fitted devices called paravanes to some ships for clearing these mines. A false nose-piece was lowered down from the stem of the vessel with two paravanes, almost like seaplanes in shape, attached to it by serrated wires. These swung outwards as the ship moved forward and the teeth on the wires cut the cables which anchored the mines so that they were cut loose and floated to the surface, where they could be exploded by rifle-fire.

We were also kept busy removing anti-mine devices from other merchant ships. Degaussing gear had been fitted to these to defeat the magnetic mines which the Germans had scattered all over the North Sea. It looked like a bunch of electric wires fastened right round the ships just inside the bulwarks. After it had been fitted the ships had been taken out of dock and 'wiped', a process which had been kept a close secret. It must in some way have stopped the magnetic mines from being attracted to the steel of the ship. I don't know how it worked but it wasn't easily removed.

We had to stop building standard ships after the war and those which were partly built had to be altered to conform to the requirements of Lloyd's and much of this work fell to me. But most of our work in 1919 consisted of altering ships from wartime to peacetime duties. I had to put the skylights back on the *Brocklesby* and the *Killingholme*, which then returned to the Humber Ferry Service. Next we had a number of German ships to repair and make ready for normal work. Two of them, the *Incular* and the *Indianola*, had had the hatches taken off and the decks made ready for carrying seaplanes. The hatches were all stowed in the holds, and I had the job of putting them back.

Then we had two passenger liners from Germany, the *Higoma* and the *Zefflin*. The *Higoma* was a medium-sized ship with a laundry on board, and a man to look after the plants, flowers and ferns. The other was a new ship with a new cruiser stern, and square windows in the deckhouse, and she too was a passenger ship.

The Germans were excellent shipbuilders. These two ships were chartered by the Wilson Line, and were claimed by the government as reparation for our losses during the war. We were later to pay dearly for this 'reparation', as the Germans were busy building a new German fleet whilst our shipyards were closing down for lack of orders.

Then in February we had our first official strike: the only one
in which I was ever involved. We struck because work and wages
were to be assessed by a process which was the forerunner of the
modern time-and-motion study methods. The idea was that a price-
fixer watched a man do a job, timed him with a stop-watch to see
how much he could do in an hour, then based the price on the
results. As we were the only tradesmen in the shipyards working
on piecework, and had been since 1894, we refused to accept the
new method, and had to strike, as the employers insisted that it
should apply to all trades. The others accepted the terms and
went back to work, but the Boilermakers' Society stayed on strike
alone, and since its members consisted of platers, burners,
caulkers, fettlers and testers, the rest of the men were soon stopped,
as we were the men who built the ships.

In the end we won, or rather we had our own way and still
worked to a price-list, but no one really wins a strike. The time
and wages lost can never be recovered. This particular strike lasted
about six weeks, and as I was paying my mother £1 5s 6d a week
for board, that took nearly all my savings. I never missed paying
her, but it was hard to see the money I was saving for my marriage
dwindle to almost nothing.

All apprentices like me received letters from the firm telling us
that we had broken our apprenticeships. We were not indentured.
If we had been they could not have had us doing piecework. We
were in a difficult position, for the Boilermakers' Society of which
we were all members insisted on our staying out, as the firm was
trying to use us to break the strike. It assured us that we would
complete our apprenticeships: a promise which was kept, since
the Society refused to settle the strike unless we were all taken
back.

It was about this time that oxy-acetylene gas was first used for
cutting holes in steel. The oxygen came in cylinders, and the gas
was made on the job from carbide. Occasionally it caused fires
when sparks ignited the acetylene generator. Electric welding was
beginning to come in, too, but only for small jobs and fittings, as it
was inclined to be brittle, and was unsuitable for general com-
bustion. The yard sent one apprentice away to be taught how to
burn with the oxy-acetylene and another to be taught welding.
Hand-riveting had almost stopped, and pneumatic or air-driven
machines were used. Drilling was done by pneumatic machines as

well and sometimes even by hydraulic or water-powered drills. But these were awkward to use as they had to be slung on a hand crane and so were only practical for certain parts of the ship. All shell-plates were scraped and planed to make a neat finish. If a plate had to be bent at right angles, a new process called 'flanging' was introduced. At first, steel was ordered especially for this process, as it involved the plate being bent in a hydraulic machine. Under pressure poor plates often cracked or broke; but as steel improved in quality more and more flanging was done instead of riveting angle bars. It gave the plate greater strength when the edge was loose and was lighter to handle and cheaper to buy.

The shapes of ships were changing too. They were now much finer fore and aft which gave them increased speed and better seaworthiness, as it cut out much of the pitching when at sea, and the extra speed helped to diminish the rolling. Some of the older types had been poor sea-going vessels. The *Marengo*, for instance, was a bad ship for pitching, and came in twice without her funnel and bridge, and with nearly everything on deck washed away.

Liz and I decided to get married in 1919, as I was earning enough. Things seemed to be looking up in the trade, and the board I was paying would just as well contribute to our own home. We were married on Easter Saturday, 19 April, at St. Mary's Roman Catholic Church on Holderness Road, by Canon Murphy. It was just a small wedding, and we went to my mother's house for tea. I wore a navy blue serge suit, and my wife had a pale blue dress and hat to match. My hat was one of the hard-crowned kind called a billycock. We were the first of our gang to marry, and all of us attended each other's weddings. I never regretted it. My wife was a good woman, who thought more of her children than she did of herself, and was still worrying about them until she died.

Most people were married at holiday times or weekends, as no one could afford to take a day off work, and going away for a honeymoon was almost unknown among working people. We had to live with my parents for six weeks until we acquired a house. When we did it was in a poor district and supposed to be rough but we never had any trouble all the time we were there. We moved to a better area seven years later, and the only difference I noticed was that in the better district neighbours watched you through the curtains, whilst in the poor one they brought their chairs out and sat on the pavement to watch. The houses were open terrace dwellings, fourteen on each side, and it was surprising how well people got on with each other. In our terrace there was a black man and his family, in the days when black people were rare. He was a gentleman and a very good cricketer.

By 1920 my earnings had improved to £160 4s 6d, which was not bad for an apprentice considering that if it rained we had to go home unless we were very lucky and had an inside job, which they had always managed to find us during the war.

I remember once, when it was snowing, we all stayed at work, and next day when it was fine but cold we all went home, and were in dire trouble next morning. The manager had us all in his office and put us on day work for three days as punishment. Day work pay was 22s a day, but those were the only three days I was on day work in the whole of my five-year apprenticeship.

6 *The Depression*

By 1921 the situation in the shipyards was very bad. My apprenticeship should have finished in February, but I had to make up any time lost through absence, including the weeks during which we had been on strike, so I had fourteen more weeks to do. I did not mind this, as it meant that work was assured. In May when my apprenticeship finished the yard was on short time four days a week, and after working for a fortnight as a journeyman, I was sacked.

I had expected this, since apprentices were generally sacked when they had finished their time, but it was hard for me. I was young and unknown in any of the yards, and half the shipyard men in the district were unemployed. I tried to get work at my trade. Word would go round that a firm had a repair job to do, and we were outside the yard at 7.30 a.m., when the foreman would come out and pick the men he wanted. Naturally he picked the men he knew.

I tried this for fourteen months, during which I worked only two and a half days on a labouring job for a cousin, loading drums of oil for export. My earnings for 1921 dropped to £107 9s 9d and were made up of wages, parish relief, unemployment pay of £1 5s a week, and an odd 10s I got by making a cloth hearth rug. In fact I made several of these. By working very hard I could finish one measuring 2 × 1 yds in sixteen hours, and I was allowed to earn the 10s a week without losing the unemployment pay.

By the end of July 1921 my income had been reduced to 15s a week, on which we struggled along for six weeks. Both my wife's parents and my own helped us a great deal. My father-in-law

25. The author's future wife, Liz,
     aged 18

24. The author aged 18

26. Unemployed in the Depression

27. The oil tanker barge, *Snipe*

28. The *Maureen Eva*

would bring us a joint of beef, and cabbages and potatoes from his allotment, and my own father would give us three or four shillings when he could afford it. This was a great help, and sometimes he bought me an ounce of tobacco. We never had any new clothes. Sometimes I had a few given and the two grandmas often bought the children a coat, a dress or a pair of shoes.

Because by this time we had two daughters, I just had to apply for parish relief. When I arrived at the hall where we had to apply (the ordinary office was not big enough) I did not like to go in. I felt a failure, but I found the place full, and met quite a lot of my old shipyard workmates there: men who had earned almost twice as much as I ever did. This eased my mind a little, but I still found it hard to take.

To obtain parish relief I had to apply to the Board of Guardians. First I had to answer endless questions about why I required assistance, which was a lot of bunk because they all knew why. One of the questions was why I had left my last job. Then they asked if I had looked for work, and whether I was particular about the kind of work I was willing to do. Believe you me, I would have taken anything! Indeed, so would all the others.

The Board applied a means test, and members of the same family were expected to help one another. For instance, if one person in a household, perhaps a son or a daughter, was working he was expected to keep the father, mother and other children without any help from anywhere. Of course if you had £10 in the bank you were told to live on it for seven weeks and then apply for relief, but even this was better than the situation before the war, when applicants had to sell their pianos and jewellery, in fact had to be really destitute before they could have relief.

The Board awarded me 15s a week, 7s 6d in cash and 7s 6d on a grocery order on which were printed the goods the grocer could supply. No luxuries like bacon and eggs. Oatmeal for making porridge, flour and yeast for making bread, and margarine we could have. Butter we could not. Potatoes were allowed, but no other vegetables. The cash was for rent, coal, light and a little meat if we could squeeze a bit out of it. We were grateful. It brought our income to 30s a week for the four of us. Our rent was 7s 9d.

This parish relief continued until March 1922 when unemployment pay was stopped for six weeks, and each man was called in front of a committee for questioning at the Labour Exchange. The committee had four members: one Union man, one for the Labour Exchange, one for the Council, and one who was neutral, generally a local councillor. When I went in they were all drinking tea, and only the Labour Exchange man spoke to me. We all knew before going in that if we had been unemployed for over six months, our unemployment pay would be stopped for six weeks.

After I had been in front of the committee, I received a pink paper saying that as they were not satisfied that I was genuinely seeking work, my unemployment pay would be stopped for six weeks. This was a lot of baloney, since everybody's pay was stopped after six months. This six-week period was known as the 'gap', when we had to rely entirely on the Board of Guardians, and I had two such periods whilst I was unemployed. During these periods the Board allowed me £1 6s a week, half in cash and half in groceries, and in return I had to put in twenty-six hours' work at East Park, digging out an extension to the boating lake.

I was out looking for work morning, noon and night, going the rounds of all the firms. But most of them had notices on the gates NO MEN WANTED, and we could not even get inside to ask. The Labour Exchange was covered with posters saying, 'GET YOUR WORK THROUGH THE EXCHANGE', but I never found any work this way.

We always had to attend the Labour Exchange at a stated time, and as the police would not let us in before or after the given time there were long queues outside as well as inside. If you missed signing on, you missed a day's pay. There were times when I was frozen stiff waiting in the rain and the cold with thousands of others, for there were said to be 20,000 of us in Hull.

Work was so hard to get in the shipyards because the standard ships built as a wartime measure, and not under Lloyd's, were sold to shipowners, who also bought and chartered the greater part of the merchant fleet handed over to the Allies by the Germans as reparation under the Peace Treaty. Consequently we had a surfeit of ships at a time when there was a great slump in world trade. Meanwhile the German yards could, in time, busy themselves replacing their old merchant ships with up-to-date models, whilst our shipyards were closed and half our shipbuilders unemployed. It has made me very bitter. During the war we could not do enough for the country, but when it was over we were thrown on the scrapheap, where a good many of us stayed until the next war.

Not only the shipyards, but the factories making shells, clothing and first-aid kits for the Army, were closed down, and several small firms went out of business too, which increased the already high unemployment in the district.

One day when I went to my desk to sign on a mistake had been made in my pay slip. I had already waited over an hour, and now had to join another queue to see the supervisor, a nasty type, well known for his rudeness. I explained to him that I was 11s short, and he started to shout about scroungers on the dole thinking they owned the place. I pointed out that I could not go home and give my wife 15s to keep the four of us for a week, to which he replied that I should just have to, as he was not going to do anything about it. He said I should just have to manage. I lost my temper. I was desperate, and lunged at him across the counter, but it was too wide and I could not reach him. Then a hand was placed on my shoulder, and a policeman took me outside. 'I know, Harry, I know,' he said, 'but if you hit him, you'll be charged with assault.' So I went home with nothing. That supervisor's name was Cook, and I shall never forget it. Eventually he had to be moved, since trouble was a daily occurrence when he was about. The men were sick of him, and he might well have caused a riot if left on the job.

The police in Hull were always good to the unemployed as far as their duties would allow. The clerks, on the other hand, were very curt and unhelpful, or just plain nasty. They treated the men signing on as if they were beneath them, whilst in reality even the clerks applying for the dole were often better qualified than they were, and amongst the unemployed were some of the best crafts-men in England. In later years when the slump eased off a much better type of clerk was in charge, and things were far more comfortable, but nothing could take away the wretchedness of being out of work.

Men who had been unemployed for long periods were very unhappy and dejected, and began to lose hope of ever finding a permanent job. Those years were well named the Depression, for that was the general feeling among all of us. Some tried to make the best of a bad job, but it needed a very strong will to ward off the general feeling of hopelessness. A few gave way to anger, which did not help either, but it did cause many men to become Communist in their thinking.

The Depression

My income for 1922 dropped to £75 16s 10d so in October I made up my mind to go all out for any job at all, labouring or anything. I tried to become a dustman, but that was impossible without the backing of one or two councillors. The same held good for bus conducting, for that again, you had to know someone. I put my name down for a job on the buses, and as far as I know it's still on the list!

On one occasion a man wanted workers for breaking up railway wagons and as I was used to handling hammers I thought I stood a chance, but he looked at our hands and if they were soft rejected us. How he expected us to have hard hands after months, even years of unemployment, I don't know.

I started to roam around the docks, where there was sometimes casual work. The foreman picked men out of the crowd every morning on the quayside, and we were paid every night. Unless the foreman, known as 'the Cod', or sometimes even 'the god', told us to report next morning, we had to stand in the crowd again and be 'chosen'. I soon found out that I only got a job when they were really pushed, as most of the men had been picked in pubs and clubs the night before. This happened all over the docks, and since I was a teetotaller I was completely out of touch. Still, I managed to get odd days and half days—mostly on jobs that the regular dockers didn't like.

One of these was shovelling sulphur into baskets, which were then pulled up from the hold and emptied into lighters. No wonder the dockers didn't like the work! They advised me to make a mask from an old sock. First I had to cut off the foot and sew in a tin lid punctured with holes so that I could breathe without inhaling too much of the dust and then I had to sew tapes to the open end so that the mask could be tied over my nose and mouth. It wasn't very successful. The sulphur dust got into our eyes and worked itself out at night in tears. We couldn't see to read, our eyes were so bad. The same sock protected our lungs when we were filling cotton seed and when we were working with copper ore which was very heavy and had a poisonous dust. Filling sacks of wheat by hand with a scuttle was another dusty job dockers didn't like, so we could do that; another was unloading pit-props. My father got this job for me. He told me that the foreman was a friend of his so I went along and was lucky. I got three days' work and sometimes more at a time, according to the size of ship we were unloading. The rough heavy props made my shoulder bleed every night in spite of the pads my wife made me out of old shirts. After a time, my shoulder had a hole in it as big as a half a crown but I was warned not to change shoulders. One sore shoulder was better than two. I wore the pad of linen, stuffed with cotton wool and soaked in carbolic oil under my shirt and stuck it out until my shoulder hardened up. That took nearly a month. I didn't dare to stay away from work. I would have lost the job.

Ordinary pay at the prop-yards was the same as that of the dockers, 7s 8d a day with an extra penny a day for some jobs. Sometimes I even managed a few days' easier work in the prop-yard, sorting the props into different lengths and stacking them. Then the foreman chose nine men to go with him across the Humber to their yard at Immingham to load wagons. This did not involve carrying the props, just counting and stowing them. I did this for five weeks—five whole weeks of work! We had to be up at 5 a.m. to catch the ferryboat to New Holland and the train to Immingham to be there for eight o'clock. We finished at 5 p.m. and were home by 7.30. There was no extra pay, just the usual wage and a shilling a day for fares. It couldn't last. I found that my father had been buying the foreman beer in the club, so I told him he had to stop. I just couldn't work under those conditions, so I finished with the props, and the foreman had to get his beer from someone else.

After that I only managed the odd day or half a day on the docks. Once I started work on a ship with 3,000 tons of maize, thinking I was all right for a full week, but at dinner time I got my ticket, a slip of paper signed by the foreman to take to the office for my pay. I had a sandwich in my pocket, so I ate it whilst I walked around looking for another job. At one o'clock I got started on a ship with 1,500 tons of grain, again expecting to get two or three days out of it, but at 5 p.m. I got my ticket again: twice in one day, and two offices to go to for my pay. I was only 'sacked' in each case because the ship's regular gang had finished the ship they were working and had been transferred to mine. It was right that they should be given preference over us, but I still claim that getting dismissed twice in one day is a record!

The pay for a morning's work on the maize ship was 3s 10d and the same for the afternoon on the wheat ship. For the first day or half-day that I worked in each week, 10d was always deducted for a National Insurance stamp, so if I had only half a day's work in a week, I was out of pocket, as I had 4s 4d a day on the dole. All the same I never refused the half-day jobs, hoping that they might lead to more work. Twice I was caught out by doing this, since two jobs I found lasted only half a day and as that was the only work I had in the week, I was 1s 4d worse off. This method of getting sacked was known as getting 'shaved' and was frequent.

If the Labour Exchange sent us for a half-day, we had to go anyway, or else our unemployment pay would be stopped for six weeks for refusing a job. Quite a few employers would ring the Exchange for a man for one afternoon. This was one of the conditions that made men angry, as a man with three or four children stood to lose more than 1s 4d a week, unemployment pay being based on so much for man and wife and so much for a child.

I was getting very tired of this haphazard method of earning a living, and desperately wanted to find something regular. I had no thoughts of following my own trade any more. By now it was 1923, and my income had improved a little to £94 17s 1d. I had got to know one or two lads on the docks who did not drink, and so was picking up a little more work, mainly on loading ships. This required more skill than unloading, since a stevedore is held responsible if a cargo moves at sea.

I remember being in the hold of a Wilson ship loading for India when the lad shouted down, 'Twenty bags of oil!' I thought he was joking—but he wasn't. They were the settlings of the linseed oil vats after it had been boiled. They were large bags, 5 ft long and full of a very stiff jelly.

We had to load a variety of cargoes from machinery, donkey boilers, railway engines and carriages to frozen meat, mostly beef and mutton. Once it was crates full of frozen rabbits, and another time 150 concrete piles 25 ft long for India.

Although I was unemployed, I was never unoccupied. I did a lot of paper-hanging and painting, and any odd jobs my relations and friends wanted doing, which earned me a few shillings and helped us out a lot. But sometimes if we had half a day to spare, my friend Jim Smallwood and I would go to East Park for a game of bowls. It was a penny an hour for the unemployed.

Towards the end of 1923 I met a plater I knew who had become a foreman at a ship-repairing yard. He could not offer me a job at my trade, but did give me a job as a plater's helper. It was still casual work, but instead of lasting just a day or half a day the work sometimes went on for four or five weeks, depending on the amount of repairs to be done.

Then I had another stroke of luck. I met Mad Jack again. He was a leading plater at another yard, and seeing me standing for a job outside the gates, he asked if I would go plater's helping for him.

Since my father-in-law was leading hand at yet another repair firm, between the two I was doing rather better, and getting experience of dock repairs. We had to repair ships whilst they were still in the dock discharging their cargo, as well as in dry docks. I went plater's helping with a plater who was making steel platforms and ladders and boiler seats for a firm at Saltend. I scaled two boilers for survey, and had to work Christmas Day and Boxing Day to get them ready in time. It was piecework, and I earned £5 in three days, which was spent on food and Christmas presents for the family.

I stayed around the shipyards until May 1924, when I got a job at East Hull Gas House which lasted seventeen weeks. I painted gas holders and sheds, did repairs, helped the fitters, served coke and tar, helped to make and bag sulphate of ammonia and clean out the boiler flues and the tunnel which went under the road to the chimney. I was always covered with fine dust—black dust this time. I was getting to be an expert on dust. For some mains we syphoned the water off by turning a tap to let the gas blow the water out, during which process we contrived to swallow a great deal of gas, but it never seemed to do me any harm, though I must admit that the men who had been working among the gas all their lives looked rather yellow. Still, they were seldom ill.

I also worked in the filter beds. There the gas was forced through oxide, which caked after a time, and had to be dug out with picks and shovels. We were swallowing gas every time we released a pocket of it. If one of us felt sleepy we were taken out into the fresh air and given a lemon squash to make us belch.

Sometimes I helped furnace bricklayers who were building a new bed of retorts. I had to make three tons of fireclay and then carry the firebricks in to them. Firebricks were made in different shapes, each of which had a different number, and the bricklayer would shout, 'Half a dozen number ones!' These I had to sort out of a heap of 20 tons which had been dumped by a tipper lorry. I did my best to have them all ready, but the job was finished before the sorting, as I had to keep two bricklayers supplied. However, they must have been satisfied, because they asked me to go abroad with them on a job which would last twelve months. It was in Spain. I thought about it, and had a talk with my wife, but as it would have meant leaving her and my two daughters, I decided against it.

That job finished in late 1924 and I had to start looking for work again. Hull Corporation was building houses in large numbers, and I got a job making breeze blocks for one of the contractors. It was very hard work and men were leaving every day. They said it was slavery, and so it was, but when one man left, there were two ready and waiting to step into his place. Near starvation is a great incentive! I stuck it for two years, and then it was the job that finished—not me.

Next I worked as a fitter's labourer in a shipyard on nights for three weeks, and when that finished, a cousin of my wife's offered me a job with his employer as a builder's labourer. It looked as if my shipbuilding days were over. I had no pride left and I jumped at the chance of a regular job. His boss was in partnership with another man, and when I arrived on the site for my first morning one of the partners came straight over to me and shook hands. He had been one of my labourers in the shipyard when I was an apprentice. Positions were reversed!

Another labourer on the site was a boilermaker who, like me, had had to take anything he could get to live. It was hard work, but healthy, and far less tiring than those blinking breeze blocks! Inwardly, I regarded it as a temporary job until I could get something better, but I was to remain in the building trade for fourteen years, and I enjoyed it. In fact, I enjoyed any job in which I was helping to construct something.

I began by mixing mortar by hand. Then I learnt to carry the hod and look after bricklayers. In two days I was a full-blown hod-carrier. It was a job that kept me fit and developed every muscle in my body, even if it did give me a thick neck. I was quick to learn, and found it stimulating to work with men from all over the British Isles. It was much better than the Gas House, where we had never been popular, as the regular workers seemed to think we were after their jobs. The builders' labourers did not.

They were used to moving from job to job. Among them were Irish, Scots, Welsh, Geordies, Cockneys and countrymen from the villages outside Hull, all good workers, who helped each other as much as possible.

The firm had a scaffolder who had been a prisoner-of-war in Germany, and he asked for me as a mate. Scaffolding in those days was by pole and rope, so my training on the keel and in the docks came in very handy, as I could tie any knot or hitch there was, as well as splice a rope. He and I got on very well indeed, and always discussed together how best to scaffold for a building. It was he who was responsible for it, so if we didn't agree, he would say, 'We'll let the matter drop, but you're wrong all the same!'

When he had been a prisoner-of-war in Germany, he was loaned out to a farmer in a very remote place. The farmer and his wife were both elderly, so he had to run the farm almost single-handed. He was there for three and a half years, and they were very good to him. He had been ordered to sleep in the barn, but the farmer's wife would not hear of it. He had his own bedroom, and ate his meals with them. It was months after the Armistice that any attempt was made to get him home. They had forgotten about him. The farmer had always supplied him with clothes and pocket money, and when the time did come for him to leave, wanted him to stay and take over the farm. But he refused, as he had a wife and daughter in England. They were in tears when he went away, and begged him to come back with his family. I think he would have done so, but his wife had gone wrong whilst he was away. That farmer wrote to him every week that I worked with him, and kept on asking him to go back.

With his help I was becoming a competent scaffolder, and it was not long before I was scaffolding on my own. I liked it. It was interesting work and I stayed with the firm for two years until the partnership dissolved, whereupon I started to look for job number forty-six.

I worked at scaffolding for several small builders, and my earnings in 1927 were £165 7s 10½d, though in the next year they fell to £124 18s 3½d because I had less overtime. The wage was £2 12s for a forty-four-hour week, but if it rained or was freezing we could not work at all. We could sign on for dole at the Labour Exchange if we were out of work because of frost but not because of rain. Sometimes the foreman would stop us for rain, and we would sit in the lobby hoping it would stop before four o'clock. If it did, we would work again, though we were never paid for the time when work had been stopped. It was while I was in the building trade that our first daughter died. She was nearly nine. My wife never got over it but I had to. I went on builder's labouring for a time. I learned to dig trenches for drains and to lay the pots in them. One builder even sent two of us to his house every week to shake all the carpets for his wife! My partner used to swear about this. He said we were 'a couple of bloody Mary Anns'.

From shaking mats I graduated to labouring for the plasterers. I was often the only labourer on the site and had to phone the builder's merchants for our materials so that the plasterers were never held up. I never saw the boss until he came to pay me at the weekend. I had a penny an hour extra all the time I worked for him, though I had to argue to get it. The difficulty was that a penny an hour extra was a Union agreement for scaffolders only, and when he asked me to go with the plasterers, I pointed out that I should be losing my penny an hour. He pointed out that I should not lose 'wet time' when it rained. We agreed on a week's trial period, at the end of which he asked the plasterers if I was satisfactory. I must have been because I got that penny an hour.

When I first started with him I worked for part of a week, and earned £1 10s 11d. He gave me £1 11s and asked me for the penny change. I hadn't even a halfpenny on me, but I gave him the penny the next day—and he took it!

I had been with the plasterers a week when I found 10s too much in my pay packet. I gave it back to the boss immediately, and was told afterwards that this was one of his ways of sorting out the honest workers. Those who didn't hand it back were finished.

As well as helping the plasterers I helped to make the drives for the houses with hard core before concreting them and I was in charge of tipping the drivers who brought the rubble. I had to make each driver sign a book for his 2s tip and refuse all small loads.

We averaged a house a week for the five years that I was with him, and they were all good houses and well finished. Some of the new tenants would come and ask if I would sell them a bucket of washed sand for planting roses and other plants. I knew they would take it at night if I refused, so I charged them 6d a bucket, and they were satisfied. When I gave the boss the 10s profit, he roared with laughter and said I was a better businessman than he was. The sand was only 10s a ton to him!

Six months after the houses had been plastered we had to go back and fill in any cracks which had appeared in the plaster. There were always a few, caused by the shrinkage of the wood, and sometimes by the tenants themselves. It was my job to decide which was which, and to report to the boss. He always left me to tell the tenants if the damage was their fault. I thought he should have done that himself, but he was strictly honest. If I wanted a halfpenny, I got it, whereas many firms paid only to the nearest halfpenny—in their favour.

In 1929 I found a job with Siemen Brothers laying cables for Hull Corporation. But it only lasted for two years and then I was unemployed again, so had to go back to the breeze blocks.

Then our third daughter was born and things began to improve. I went back to the building trade and by 1938 I was earning £159 16s 5d and had worked on many important buildings in Hull including the New Theatre.

In 1939 war broke out and all of a sudden there was a demand for shipyard men again. I hardly dared to hope that I might get back to ships. The day I rejoined the Boilermakers' Union there were only six of the thirty-two apprentices who had served their time with me still working at their trade, and I thought then that there was something wrong with a world in which there had to be a war before a man could do his job. I had had over forty different jobs from 1922 to 1938.

Two of the foremen in repair yards promised me a job but I had to wait. Meanwhile my younger daughter was sent to Selby in a mass evacuation. After three weeks my wife went to see her, and found that she was fretting and was clearly ill. She brought her home and sent for the doctor, who diagnosed scarlet fever. Then of course we did not want to send her back, but we knew Hull would be bombed, so after a long talk with my wife it was decided that I should try for a job I had seen advertised at a small shipyard in Thorne, of all places, where we should be safe from the bombing. And so, twenty years after leaving the town to earn my apprenticeship and make my fortune, I found myself back in Thorne.

7 *Shipbuilding again*

I had found myself a job in one of the old keelbuilding yards where in my childhood I had spent so many happy hours, and at last I was able to make ships again, building not keels but barges and tugs, which were launched into the same canal that I had sailed so often as a lad.

I had an Aunt Polly living in Thorne, and although I had not seen her for twenty years and had no idea where she lived, I hoped to persuade her to take me as a lodger. On my way from the station to the town, I met her husband, Uncle Dick, himself an old keelman, and he took me home with him. Aunt Polly was a lively little woman in her sixties. She was delighted to see me, and declared she would be offended if I stayed anywhere else. She had always been a hard worker, and would have a go at anything. She was turned seventy-five when she took her first trip in an aeroplane and asked the pilot to loop the loop for her.

I started work at Dunston's shipyard the following Monday. I was nervous. Eighteen years is a long time to be away from your trade, and the work was quite different from that of my early training. The yard was much smaller, employing less than a hundred men and making mainly river barges and small tugs. The men were rather unfriendly too. They were all locals and seemed to be afraid that outsiders might take away their jobs. The war was, of course, making more shipyard work available, and labour was moving about. Still, I was the first 'foreigner' at the yard.

I had told the manager how long I had been away from my trade, and that I had no experience of barge building, but the foreman did not improve matters by giving me as a helper a young man called Ray Milner who had never before set foot in a shipyard. He had been a bus conductor.

Another difficulty was the shortage of tools. The foreman's advice was to borrow if I could, but no offers were forthcoming. I had small tools of my own, but shipyards usually supplied large ones. That first Monday was the most uncomfortable I have ever spent.

We got through it somehow, and my helper was not long in picking up the job, nor in telling the men what he thought of their attitude towards us. I soon found that my skill as a craftsman had not left me, and after a fortnight on minor jobs for two barges, we seemed to be on our feet. However, I discovered that small vessels were just as difficult to build as big ones, since the same shape and curve had to be achieved in about a fifth of the length. There was just not as much of the straight, and easier, work in the middle. Then the manager put me on shell-work for an ocean-going tug. This consisted of marking off the plates for the curved hull of the ship, a job most platers loathed. I found I could do it with ease, and my confidence returned. The men began to get more friendly too. They had found out that I had been born in Thorne. All was forgiven. I soon began to feel at home, as indeed I was.

Dunston's had changed since its keelbuilding days. It had launched the last wooden keel in 1922, and now built a variety of steam- and diesel-powered craft ranging from barges and tugs to lighters and coasters. All these vessels were of steel, so drilling, punching and shearing machines had been installed and a furnace built for heating and shaping the steel plates and bars. The whole yard had electric motors to work the machinery, instead of steam engines, and the three wooden sheds with their old-fashioned pantile roofs held countersinking machines, radial drills and the joggling machine, as well as the rollers, the punching and shearing machines and eventually a new hydraulic press. The old sail loft had been converted into offices, but the ropery no longer made rope, though the old ropewalk was still there.

Even the workmen had changed. Carpenters had become shipwrights, and there was a new breed of riveters, platers, welders, caulkers, engineers, loftsmen and draughtsmen.

But shipbuilding itself had changed surprisingly little in the years I had been away from my trade. The biggest adjustment for me was that, as Dunston's was a smaller yard than Earle's, the platers did not work in squads, each squad specializing in a different part of the ship, but on their own with perhaps one helper, and were sometimes responsible for the entire ship. The work was more varied and interesting because of this and you had to be an all-round plater.

In Earle's on the other hand, the platers worked in squads. First the shell squad built the keel. Then the shipwrights took over and laid it out so that it was dead straight and level. Next the framing squad built the centre keelson—a centre girder running from end to end of the ship and fixed to the keel and the floors from either solid plates or skeleton bars. The floors were built outwards from the centre line to the bilges, the rounded part of the ship from the bottom up to the sides. The same squad made the frames or ribs of the ship but a beam squad made the beams which stretched across the ship from frame to frame to carry the decks.

A hatch and girder squad made the longitudinal girders and the hatchsides or coamings, while a deck squad made the deck plates, and a shell squad made the outside of the ship or the shell. There had even been a stern squad which made only the aft ends of ships.

The deckhouses and casings which covered the engine rooms were made inside the platers' shops, as were the bulkheads which divided the ship transversely. They were only taken to the ship when complete and ready for erecting.

In Dunston's platers were expected to mark off for every part of the ship and in my eighteen years there I reckon I did them all in their turn. Marking off was done in the same way as before, although more and more templates were made by loftsmen in the mould loft rather than by platers. Blueprints changed too; they became black drawings on a white background instead of white on blue.

Punching and shearing were unchanged but plates could not be scarphed or planed. Instead there was a 'joggling' machine at Dunston's which bent a plate so that it overlapped the next one and tapered packings of steel were used to fill the gaps.

Frames in Earle's had been heated in a furnace and bent to shape with hydraulic rams but in Dunston's the frames had to be bent by hand with bending 'weazes'.

Hand-riveting had completely disappeared and all riveting was

126

done with hand-held, pneumatic machines, and because the ships we made were smaller, the hatchsides and side decks were made in one piece and bent at right angles in rollers, although later we did get a flanging machine to do this.

The yard itself was fifty-seven miles from the sea, and all boats had to be launched sideways into the canal. Of course the yard was restricted as to the size of ship it could build because of the depth of the canal and the height of the fixed railway bridge beyond the yard. Still, we could manage a ship up to 140 ft in length, as that length could still negotiate the sharp corners in canals and rivers, but we couldn't make the ship's beam more than 22 ft because of the limitations of the canal, and of Keadby Lock, which led from the canal into the Trent and then into the Humber: my old route in fact. The fixed railway bridge did not affect us much. We could, and did, complete all the superstructure after passing ships under the bridge.

The traffic on the canal was not very different from that in my day. Of course there were no sails any more. I watched steel-built, diesel-powered barges ploughing their way past me carrying wheat from Hull to the flour mills at Doncaster, Mexborough, Rotherham and Sheffield, and general goods, or steel ingots, for the rolling mills at Rotherham, Tinsley and Sheffield. On their return journey they still carried coal from the collieries to Hull or Flixborough on the Trent, where Lysaghts had a wharf to supply their steelworks. The coal trade to Hull was dying slowly as more and more trawlers were converting to oil burning and diesel engines, although there was still a little going to Hull Gas House and to wharves on the river Hull for general use.

However, there were one or two wooden keels still in use— fitted with engines of course. One called the *Gondolier* was powered by a single-cylinder Scandinavian engine. We could hear it coming a mile away. 'There's Old Bumper coming!' we used to say. The pistons used to shake the aft deck, and the man steering looked as if he was dancing. Its noise rattled the drawing office windows and some say it even blew six-inch smoke-rings from its exhaust.

Sometimes I even got a wave or a shout from old keelmen who remembered me. The Holts and the Deans still worked the canals, but their wives and children no longer lived aboard.

One or two keels were still in use on the Humber too. They were used to carry barrage balloons. The towns of Grimsby and

Hull were, of course, both open to the river, and Hull had a seven-mile front to defend, so inland barrage balloons were of little use. The keels were based at Immingham on the Lincolnshire side of the Humber. They were useful because they could get in and out of the dock at any time and at any state of the tide. They had keelmen for their captains and mates and servicemen to look after the balloons. They were put out into the river inside the defence booms at dusk as most air-raids were at night. The defence booms across the Humber were closed at dusk so that no submarines, or any kind of shipping could get in or out. The booms were a double row of piles driven into the river bed, each with torpedo nets stretched between them. If a submarine got through the first she still had to negotiate the second, but none ever did. No doubt the Germans knew all about them anyway. During the day an opening in each boom was made by a steam tug to allow shipping to move about the river and naval ships were moored to buoys just inside the booms.

Thorne itself had changed very little in the years from 1915 to 1939. South Parade had become a wide main road, and the grass verges had disappeared. It was no place for a gipsy horse-fair any more. An iron swing-bridge had replaced the wooden one over the canal, as the old one had a load limit of 5 tons, which was no use for the increasingly heavy traffic on the main road from Hull and Goole to Doncaster and the south of England.

There were two new housing estates in the town, and a pit village at Moorends where the colliery had been sunk. The town centre, however, was exactly the same, with the old pump at the corner of the market place, and the church at the top of our only hill, with its tithe barn still standing. Even the old Church School was still there and in use.

The old workhouse had become a barracks for a battalion of Scots. They looked very smart on the march with their pipes and drums. They went to North Africa. Much later another regiment, The Royal Sussex, came and my elder daughter eventually married one of them.

The Hall, the home of the Foster family, had been turned into the Council Offices and its fields where we had held our sports had become the town's park, complete with a bandstand, pond, paddling pool, war memorial, and sheep to keep down the grass and help the war effort.

128

29. Tom Puddings on the canal at Stainforth

30. The sideways launching of a large Tom Pudding at Dunston's

31. Staniland's keelbuilding yard at Thorne

33. The author aged 75 with
    Dunston's yard in the
    background

32. The author aged 65 at
    the Yorkshire Dry Dock
    Company Yard

Staniland's, the other keelbuilding yard, was still there, but had turned to building cabin cruisers, pleasure boats and yachts. The old pitchponds of the tar works had become their yachting basin and was full of yachts, put in there for the winter and the war. During the war the yard was mainly employed in repairing wooden barges.

The population of Thorne had expanded as well as changed. There were miners from Durham and Scotland working in the new pit, and even a bus service bringing in people from Doncaster and Goole, and allowing us to travel abroad to their shops and markets.

Anxious to get my family away from Hull before the air-raids started in earnest, I began looking for a house, and eventually was given the chance of a cottage with a large garden stretching down to the fields bordering the canal. The middle one of three farm cottages, it had been practically rebuilt by the owner, a farmer with a reputation for meanness; but though we lived in his house for eighteen years, we never found him mean. The rent was weekly, but our new neighbours told us he only collected it when he had to pay a bill, and he did too. Sometimes he left it for three months, and I thought he was taking a risk, as he did not know us, but I was wrong about that, since he had inquired about our family from Thorne people who had known my father, and had spoken to my employer before letting us the house.

I arrived with our furniture on Easter Tuesday 1940, and had to leave the van parked outside the farmer's house while I collected the key. He was amazed to hear that I had brought my furniture. 'What if I'd changed my mind?' he said. I told him I had taken his word, and he laughed and said farmers were used to taking a man's word as his bond.

But there was another hold-up. The driver of the van, who lived near us in Hull, refused to unload any furniture until he had inspected the house. He knew my wife had not seen it, and said if he hadn't thought she would like it he would have driven straight back to Hull.

Of course we were thankful to be in the cottage after the air-raids in Hull, but it was a shock for my wife. She was used to electricity, and we had had an electric cooker, kettle, wireless and lights. In our new cottage we had gas lighting, a wireless set run from a battery, and worst of all, a dry lavatory some yards from the house. It was an earth closet, not by any means unusual in Thorne at that time, but my wife never stopped campaigning for water closets. She told the drainage inspector that Thorne was fifty years behind the rest of the world, and he always nodded to her after that. She got her water closets too—eventually.

The cottage was small but comfortable, and very cosy in winter. In summer we could sit outside at the back and see nothing but gardens and fruit trees. The neighbours too were friendly and pleasant. They both turned out to be distantly related to us. Everybody in Thorne seemed to be!

Our garden was a mess, and there were 750 sq yds of it in contrast to the 6 sq yards I had left in Hull. By the end of the summer I had it in good shape. Later I built a greenhouse and two cold frames, and later still a chicken house for six chickens. We had apple, pear and plum trees, gooseberry, redcurrant and blackcurrant bushes, and lots of rhubarb. We were never without fresh fruit, and my wife was always making fruit pies and jam. Eventually I grew tomatoes and cucumbers, and even my own tobacco.

My yearly earnings now ranged from £151 5s 1d in 1939 to £683 in 1944 but that was, of course, largely due to the war bonus, for work came in fast during the war and at one time the yard employed nearly 210 men.

Before 1942 most vessels had been of riveted construction, but after that more and more electric welding took over. This meant that the processes of punching, riveting, countersinking and joggling were no longer necessary. Gas-cutting eventually did away with the need for shearing too, and so shipbuilding became much simpler.

Dunston's were the pioneers in making all-welded craft of the smaller type. I remember the first T.i.d.s. (Tidworth Class tugs). These were small steam-tugs to work on the canals and rivers, and they had no names, just numbers. They were built in five sections, which were welded together. Some of them had even been made in inland plating shops in Lancashire and Lincolnshire, brought by road to Dunston's, welded together and launched into our canal. At one time we were launching a tug a week and I was paying income tax for the first time in my life.

We once built some oil carriers for naval stations overseas, and as they were far too big to go down the canal, we simply built them and then took them down again, and sent each part carefully marked, by road to Liverpool. They were re-erected in Malta and Gibraltar.

We even built ships in two halves and floated them down the river to the firm's other yard at Hessle on the Humber, where they were put together and launched. They were big water-carriers.

Sometimes we built strange things like wood and steel targets for aircraft bombing practice. These were built, taken to pieces and sent by road to be re-assembled on the beaches of South Wales, where they were launched and anchored off the coast.

But perhaps the most unusual jobs done in our shipyard were those carried out by a section of the Royal Engineers, who had to adapt two tanks for the invasion. One was to be used for laying metal as temporary landing strips for aeroplanes. The other was for exploding landmines—and a queer sight it was! It had a cylinder covered with flailing chains held out in front by two long arms. Of course we all offered our advice, helpful and otherwise, but the jobs were done. The tank drivers had been bakers in civilian life, and their sergeant had been a butcher. The Engineers stayed with us for a while, making sections for Bailey bridges, and then left, presumably for D-day and Normandy.

When the Second World War was over my earnings fell to £493 13s in 1946, for the yard was returning to peacetime work, and of course fewer ships were needed. The situation was by no means as bad as after the First World War, since some of the men drafted into shipbuilding returned to their civilian jobs, and so eased the pressure a little.

We finished off some of the ships we had on order, the 'puffers', tugs and barges, because they could be used for peacetime jobs. The 'puffers' were small steamships called 'puffers' because they 'puffed' away like railway engines. They were intended to be used for carrying supplies from the shore to the Royal Navy vessels at anchor in Scapa Flow, and so were designed for the Caledonian Canal and the Scottish locks. We built ten of them, and they were eventually sold to a private owner.

Next we turned to building swim barges for the Thames, and tugs to tow them. But by then Dunston's yards were becoming very well known for their bulk-construction methods, that is building ships in sections and then welding them together. They even built sections of some vessels upside down to get downhand welding, which made the welding better and easier to do, and what's more, began to build them inside new fabrication sheds. This meant that a complete ship could be made away from the launching berths and not assembled there until the vessel was almost ready to be launched.

While I was at Dunston's they also developed a new type of barge with semi-straight lines. They were easier to build, lighter to use, and cheaper to buy than the traditional barge, and became very popular. Because they had no round bilges they needed no furnace work, and for the same reason they were able to carry more cargo. The first we built was called the *Dunham*, and it was so successful that orders came in thick and fast.

Many of the barges we made were still 'Sheffield size', just as the old keels had been, because some of the locks on our canals had not been altered since my sailing days and if a barge was made for the Sheffield run it had to be Sheffield size.

In 1948 the firm made the first all-welded tug with the curved lines of a ship instead of the semi-straight lines of the all-welded T.i.d. tugs. It was a big step from an all-welded barge to a tug, but again it was successful, so in 1949 the firm took a bigger step, and made the first all-welded fishing vessel. This was a sea-going trawler, but it was made at the Hessle yard.

I helped to make the first trawlers we ever built at Thorne. They were part-riveted, part-welded, and had to have their super-structure taken down and refitted beyond the railway bridge. They even went to Hull to have their engines put in, then came back to Thorne to be completed. With a squad of labourers I was left about a mile from the yard to refit the engine casings and all the work above deck with a one-legged hand crane. These trawlers were built for Lowestoft, and their owners were very pleased with them.

I enjoyed making anything, even unusual vessels like the push barges for Africa. They carried coal in the holds, and the hatch covers rolled off sideways, so that when the hold was full the hatches could be put back and rails erected at the sides, so that cattle could be herded on top. They even had seats for passengers in the deckhouses. They had two large push posts at each end so that they did not have to be turned round, and were pushed by power units at the back. They were the ugliest craft I ever built.

When finished, they were taken down, parcelled up, taken to

132

Liverpool and shipped to Africa. They had to be painted in different colours so that the Africans could rebuild them there. No. 1 was painted red for the portside and green for starboard, and instructions were stencilled and clearly stamped on the sections. To make sure that the various halves were not mixed up No. 2 had brown for port and blue for starboard, and No. 3 yellow and white.

We also made sugar barges for the West Indies. They were 60 ft long, 14 ft wide and 8 ft deep, and were built completely, then lifted in one piece and taken to Liverpool, and carried on the deck of a cargo ship. They were so awkward on the roads that they had to have a police escort—a truly 'abominable' load, as my son-in-law called them.

I was happy at Dunston's. I was even the foreman plater there for a short time, with 19 platers, 5 apprentices, 5 burners, 24 platers' helpers, 2 cranedrivers and a countersinker in my department. But I didn't like being a foreman. I preferred building ships, and went on building them at Paull, by the side of the Humber, and at Yorkshire Dry Dock on the river Hull, where Ray Milner, my first apprentice at Dunston's came into my life again—this time as my foreman.

Now I have retired and am back once again where I was born. Thorne has changed a little. There's a permanent road bridge over the canal now and even a marina where the keels once moored for the night. But the inscription, 'RAYNERS CYCLE WORKS', is still to be seen on the roofs of the shops in the Market Place, just as it was when I was a baker's boy. That must have been a drop of good enamel!

The pit at Moorends has closed and the miners are 'bussed' away to work, but the shipyard is still there and thriving. It employs about 128 men now and makes tugs and trawlers as well as other craft. I can hear its clanging all day long. Sometimes I take a walk along the canal bank to see what they are doing. I watch ships being built for countries as far away as Ceylon, Nigeria or Bahrain. Now and then, just as I once did as a little lad, I see the occasional barge loaded with wheat going to the flour mills at Rotherham, and yachts and pleasure boats going along the canal to the Trent, then into the Humber, and from the Humber perhaps even to the sea.

Appendix One BY L. T. C. ROLT

Yorkshire Keel Canals and River Navigations

Map 1

	Miles	Furlongs
R. Humber: Hull to Trent Falls	18	0
R. Hull: Struncheonhill Lock to Hull	20	0
Driffield Nav.: Driffield to Struncheonhill Lock	7	0
Driffield Nav.: Frodingham & Corps Landing Branches	3	2
Market Weighton Nav.: Old Sod House Lock to Humber	6	0
R. Ouse: Trent Falls to Swale Nab	60	6
R. Wharfe: Tadcaster to York (R. Ouse)	9	2
R. Ure Nav.: Ripon to Swale Nab	10	0
R. Derwent: Malton to Barmby (R. Ouse)	38	0
Pocklington Canal to Cottingwith Ferry (R. Derwent)	9	4
R. Aire: Asselby Island (R. Ouse) to Weeland (Aire & Calder Nav.)	12	0

Map 2

	Miles	Furlongs
Ancholme Nav.: Bishopbridge to Humber at Ferriby Sluice	19	0
R. Trent: Trent Falls as far as Torksey	36	4

Map 3

	Miles	Furlongs
Aire & Calder and Sheffield & South Yorkshire Junction Canal	5	4

Map 4

	Miles	Furlongs
Sheffield & South Yorkshire Navigations:		
Stainforth & Keadby Canal (R. Trent to R. Don at Bramwith)	12	0
R. Don Nav.: Fishlake Ferry to Tinsley	29	0
Sheffield Canal: Tinsley to Sheffield	3	7
Dearne & Dove Canal: Swinton Junc. (R. Don) to Barnsley Junc.	9	5
Elsecar Branch	2	$1\frac{1}{2}$
Worsborough Branch	2	$1\frac{1}{2}$
R. Don: Fishlake Old Ferry to Goole (R. Ouse, Yorks)	9	2
Aire & Calder Navigations:		
Goole (R. Ouse) to Castleford	24	0
Castleford to Leeds	10	0
Castleford to Wakefield	8	0
Barnsley Canal	14	2
Selby Branch	11	6
R. Aire: Selby Branch to Weeland	4	6
Dewsbury Old Cut	1	0
Calder & Hebble Nav: Fall Ing (A. & C.N.) to Sowerby Bridge	21	4
Calder & Hebble Nav.: Halifax Branch	1	6
Huddersfield Broad Canal: Cooper Bridge (C. & H.N.) to Huddersfield	3	4
TOTAL	423	3

Appendix Two

*Maps showing
the Yorkshire Keel Canals
and River Navigations*

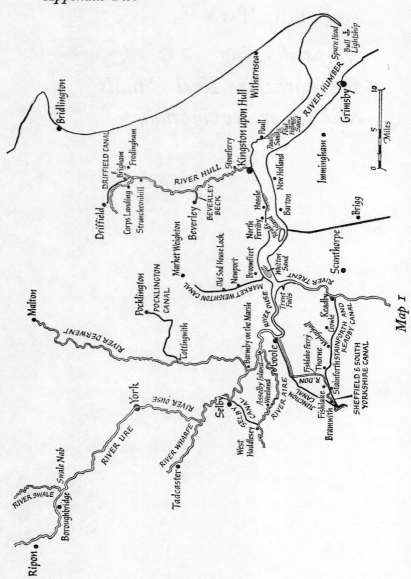

Map I

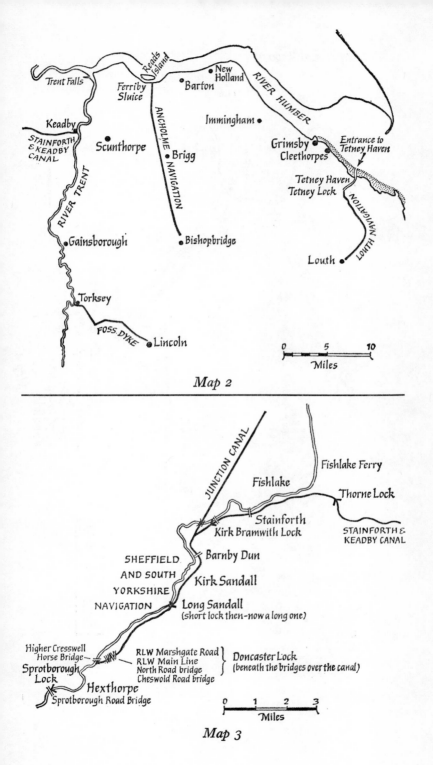

Map 2

Trent Falls
Reads Island
New Holland
Barton
Ferriby Sluice
RIVER HUMBER
Keadby
STAINFORTH & KEADBY CANAL
Scunthorpe
ANCHOLME NAVIGATION
Brigg
Immingham
Grimsby
Cleethorpes
Entrance to Tetney Haven
Tetney Haven
Tetney Lock
LOUTH NAVIGATION
RIVER TRENT
Gainsborough
Bishopbridge
Louth
Torksey
FOSS DYKE
Lincoln

0   5   10
Miles

Map 3

JUNCTION CANAL
Fishlake Ferry
Fishlake
Thorne Lock
Stainforth
Kirk Bramwith Lock
STAINFORTH & KEADBY CANAL
SHEFFIELD AND SOUTH YORKSHIRE NAVIGATION
Barnby Dun
Kirk Sandall
Long Sandall
(short lock then—now a long one)
Higher Cresswell Horse Bridge
RLW Marshgate Road
RLW Main Line
North Road bridge
Cheswold Road bridge
Doncaster Lock
(beneath the bridges over the canal)
Sprotborough Lock
Hexthorpe
Sprotborough Road Bridge

0   1   2   3
Miles

Map 3

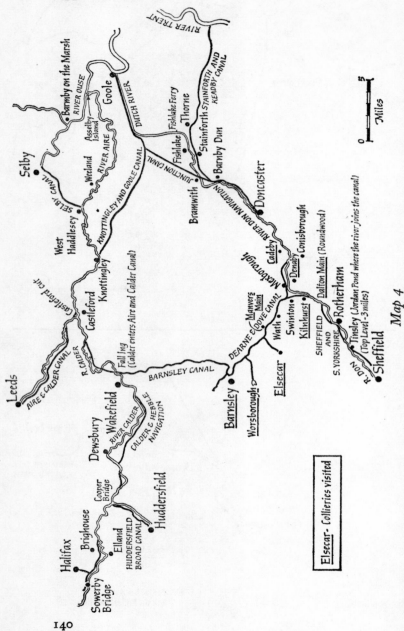

Map 4

Elsecar - Collieries visited

Notes on the Plates

Cover. Keels off St. Andrews Dock. Reproduced by kind permission of Mr Harry Cartlidge.

1. Keel *Sunbeam* on the Trent. Reproduced by kind permission of Mr Michael Jackson from a print by the late E. W. Carter.

2. Keel *Attercliffe* at Keadby (Carter Collection, Gainsborough Public Library). Reproduced by kind permission of the County Librarian, Brayford House, Lincoln.

3. Keadby lock. On the left at the coal shute below Keadby lock in the river Trent are two London spritsail barges loaded with coal. In the foreground a keel is entering Keadby lock to go into the Stainforth and Keadby canal. The sail is lying rolled up, but not under cover, on the hatches and the water cask is on the right-hand side of the keel. The big wooden tiller used in the Humber is lying on the ropes coiled on the hatch and has been replaced by an iron one for use in the canal, where there were sharper corners to negotiate. The wooden one was restricted by the stanchions and could not get far enough to port or starboard.

4a. The fore end of a wooden keel. On the left are two blocks: one is attached to a bridle fixed to the hause timbers, the other to the mainstay of the mast, and both are connected to the double purchase roller with chains or wires. These are used to erect the mast. The hause timbers with the hause pipes for anchor chains are on either side of the centrepiece which is decorated with gold leaf. The stem of the vessel can be seen and the binns with their convex iron rubbing bars. The captain is wearing the neat-fitting keelman's guernsey.

4b. Detail of the centrepiece decorated with gold leaf.

5. The *Faith* moored in Thorne 'rack'. The coggy boat has the tow-rope coiled inside it, and there is a fancy plaited fender on the

rudder. The keel has no mast or sails but the transom rail, side rails, timber heads, sheet rollers and binns with their convex iron rubbing bars can be clearly seen.

6. The wooden swing bridge at Stainforth. A keel loaded with pit props is passing through the raised wooden swing bridge. The horse hauling the keel has crossed over the bridge before it was opened and the horse-line can be clearly seen. The keel's mast has been lowered to reduce resistance to the wind and make it a bit easier for the horse.

7. The double locks at Keadby leading out of the river Trent into the Stainforth and Keadby canal. Beyond the lock is a wooden swing bridge for the road, and beyond that are three keels, one of which is unloading—it has a temporary derrick. In the background are two 'light' keels perhaps waiting to load.

8. The Aegir on the Trent—a very small one.

9. The tugs *Welshman* and *Irishman* heading towards the Trent end on the way to Hull. The *Welshman* is not towing but the *Irishman* has two tow-ropes showing, so it probably has four or six keels in tow.

10. The bridgeman's lobby at Toll Bar Bridge, Thorne, when it was a swing bridge over the canal. There is now a permanent road bridge there.

11. A keelman's wedding. The wedding carriage of a newly married couple is being pulled around the village by fellow keelmen using a man-line.

12. A wooden keel, the *Day Star*, at Docking Hill, Doncaster in 1904. She was owned by Hanley's flour mill and used for carrying grain from Hull to Doncaster. Her leeboards have not been left behind as she rarely went further than Doncaster. There is a clear view of the one on the port side.

13. A horse marine taking his horse to the stables.

14. The Old House lock half-way up the hill from Tinsley to Sheffield. It was the only one of the eight locks with a lock-keeper. Jack Schofield and his wife of Thorne have been unloading iron ingots into carts by hand. The keel has a temporary derrick. There was a steam crane there for heavy lifting but it had to be paid for. Its rails are in the foreground.

15. Stainforth Aquatic Sports Committee. The keelmen are wearing their hand-knitted guernseys.

16. Watersports at Stainforth: sculling race for keelmen's wives in the keels' coggy boats.

17. The greasy pole.

18. Keels moored at Stainforth during Fair Week. Note the height of the masts.

19. Thorne Travis Charity School. Harry Fletcher, aged nine, is second from left on the back row during one of his rare attendances.

20. Albert Dock, Hull. In the foreground are three keels, a sloop and five lighters waiting for cargo. One keel and two lighters are being loaded from the ship—a lot of sugar was loaded in this part of the dock. A trawler can be seen near the sheerlegs waiting for its engines and boiler to be lifted in. The passenger ship on the right is moored where the ships carrying Russian immigrants used to berth.

21. The 'old harbour', Hull. The wooden keel on the left is 'light', while the iron keel in the centre with three coggy boats is loaded. The tall building on the right is Rank's flour mill. The photograph shows how congested this part of the river always was.

22. Rank's flour mill near the entrance to Victoria Dock on the river Hull. The keel is loading flour to be taken up the canal to Rotherham. The lighters close to Drypool Bridge are discharging grain into the mill.

23. The author's father, 'Young Jim' (left) with a friend. Both are dressed in their Sunday best.

24. The author aged eighteen when he was an apprentice plater.

25. The author's future wife, Liz, aged eighteen.

26. Unemployed in the Depression. Reproduced by kind permission of the Radio Times Hulton Picture Library.

27. Sea trials in the Humber of the oil tanker barge, *Snipe* (diesel engines). Reproduced by kind permission of the *Hull Daily Mail*. This is one of the barges Harry Fletcher worked on while at Dunston's of Thorne.

28. The author with one of the last barges he built, the *Maureen Eva*, which is moored in the dock at Goole.

29. Tom Puddings on the canal at Stainforth waiting to be loaded with coal from Hatfield Main Colliery. They are of the old type carrying 10, 12 or 15 tons of coal.

30. The sideways launching of a large Tom Pudding at Richard Dunston's of Thorne. Two more can be seen under construction.

31. Staniland's keelbuilding yard by the canal at Thorne. The men have been building a keel for John H. Whitaker of Hull. In the foreground is a young fir, a 'ricker' or 'wricker' for making boathooks.

32. The author aged sixty-five (just before his retirement) at the Yorkshire Dry Dock Company Yard on the river Hull. On the left he and the foreman shipwright are checking the keel bar to see

that it is dead straight. The barge has been cut in half, and a 22 ft section is to be put in to lengthen it.

33. The author aged seventy-five on the hauling bank of the canal at Thorne. Dunston's shipyard is in the background.